POSSIBILITY
LIVING

POSSIBILITY LIVING

Add Years to Your Life and

Life to Your Years with

God's Health Plan

ROBERT A. SCHULLER
AND
DOUGLAS DI SIENA, D.C., F.I.C.A.

HarperSanFrancisco

A Division of HarperCollins*Publishers*

POSSIBILITY LIVING: Add Years to Your Life and Life to Your Years with God's Health Plan. Copyright © 2000 by Robert A. Schuller and Douglas Di Siena. All rights reserved. Printed in the United States of America. No part of this book may be used or reproduced in any manner whatsoever without written permission except in the case of brief quotations embodied in critical articles and reviews. For information address HarperCollins Publishers, Inc., 10 East 53rd Street, New York, NY 10022.

HarperCollins books may be purchased for educational, business, or sales promotional use. For information please write: Special Markets Department, HarperCollins Publishers, Inc., 10 East 53rd Street, New York, NY 10022.

HarperCollins Web site: http://www.harpercollins.com
HarperCollins®, ☕®, and HarperSanFrancisco™ are trademarks of
HarperCollins Publishers, Inc.

FIRST EDITION
Designed by Joseph Rutt

Library of Congress Cataloging-in-Publication Data
Schuller, Robert A.
Possibility living: add years to your life and life to your years with God's health plan / Robert A. Schuller and Douglas Di Siena.— 1st ed.
p. cm.
ISBN 0–06–067086–X (cloth)
ISBN 0–06–067085–1 (pbk.)
ISBN 0–06–067652–3 (Crystal Cathedral edition)
1.Health—Religious aspects—Christianity. I. Di Siena, Doug. II. Title.
BT732. S38 2001
248—dc21   00–032047

00 01 02 03 04 ❖/RRD(H) 10 9 8 7 6 5 4 3 2 1

CONTENTS

ACKNOWLEDGMENTS

We want to take this time to thank all who have made it possible to write this book.

First we would like the thank *God* for the inspiration and the energy to make it happen.

We want to acknowledge our wives, Donna and Mariela, for their lasting love, patience, and support. We truly appreciate their commitment to us in our efforts to spread the message of Possibility Living.

We thank our kids for their understanding, love, and support during this time, and for the times we were not able to spend with them because we gave it to this work.

We thank our staffs and colleagues for their constant support, loyalty, and prayers. To be surrounded by people of such quality, integrity, and commitment is a blessing.

We thank Dr. Larry Keefauver for his support in helping us organize our thoughts. We are grateful for his devotion and hard work in making this a reality.

We thank our agent, Lois De LaHaba, for finding the right publisher, HarperSanFrancisco, and working out the details to make the book possible.

We thank everyone at HarperSanFrancisco for their support and council. We are especially indebted to John Loudon, Roger Freet, Gideon Weil, and Terri Leonard. They helped us refine and polish this book, bringing it to its fullest potential.

Lastly, we would like to thank all of you who have purchased this book. We hope you will be an active participant in the concepts that we share. Your step into Possibility Living is our reward.

Thank you!

FOREWORD

I am extremely proud of my son, Dr. Robert A. Schuller. His foresight, knowledge, and wisdom are to be commended. He is someone you need to hear. The combination of Robert with Dr. Douglas Di Siena is one that bridges health science and religion in a unique and special way. Doug has been very helpful to me and my wife, Arvella. His gentle and loving demeanor immediately sets the tone and pace for the healing power of God to flow.

I want to encourage you to read every word. Follow the suggestions and begin the process of Possibility Living today. Some of the steps are challenging. I personally struggle with the challenge of eating as healthfully as I should. But, when I do, I notice a difference not only in my waist, but in my vitality and spirit.

I want to thank Robert and Doug for clarifying and putting into words the way I have tried to live my life. Because it is Possibility Living that gives us the ability to fulfill our God-given potential, I believe that I am in process of doing that. As a result, I believe that the next thirty years will be my best ever. Don't ever give up on life and don't ever quit. God has designed you to live a healthy, energetic, and fulfilled life. I have lived that philosophy for over seventy years. I plan on preaching and being active in the church until the day God calls me home and I challenge you to live every day with the possibilities that God is giving you.

—Dr. Robert H. Schuller

INTRODUCTION

Shoot for the Moon . . . even if you miss,
you'll be among the stars.

The purpose of *Possibility Living* is to add years to your life and life to
your years. It is our hope and prayer that through these pages you will
find knowledge and information to help you live the positive life God
has planned for you — "plans to prosper you, plans to give you hope and
a future." Following God's health plan for your life will allow you to
experience physical, emotional, and spiritual vitality.

Jesus spent his ministry communicating this reality. He began with
the spiritual. His baptism was a coronation — a time of spiritual
empowerment. He was given the gift of the Holy Spirit to protect,
guide, and strengthen him. Immediately afterward, he took the time
needed for preparation and cleansing by going into solitude for fasting
and prayer for forty days and nights.

Jesus was more that a spiritual teacher; he was a psychologist of the
finest order. He enlightened people about their potential and gave
them hope. He gave us the keys to happiness. After dinner, it is not
unusual for the family to read the Beatitudes. They were given to us by
Jesus when he prepared his Sermon on the Mount, his first recorded
sermon, delivered on a hillside by the Sea of Galilee. There, overlook-
ing this beautiful freshwater lake, Jesus told us how happiness works:

Happy are those who know they are spiritually poor . . .
Happy are those who mourn . . .
Happy are those who are humble . . .
Happy are those whose greatest desire is to do what
    God requires . . .
Happy are those who are merciful to others . . .
Happy are the pure in heart . . .

Happy are those who work for peace . . .
Happy are those who are persecuted . . .
Happy are you when people insult, persecute you and tell all
    kinds of evil lies against you.
                                                    Matthew 5:1–11

Happiness does not have its source in circumstances outside ourselves, but in the spirit of the living God within. It comes from the spiritual reality of God impacting our emotional base and creating
happiness. The goal of psychotherapy is to create happiness or peace.
Jesus gave us the key.

Jesus was the greatest physician the world has ever seen. He healed
thousands of people on a regular basis. The mistake we make in inter-
preting this history given in the Scriptures is to assume that his healing
power was miraculous and therefore not repeatable.

John Wimber, founder of Vineyard Ministries, taught at Fuller
Theological Seminary in the late 1970s and early 1980s. The only pro-
fessor without the "proper" credentials, he taught the class "Signs and
Wonders." His teaching, which became the premise of his more than
one thousand churches, is that Jesus gave us the power to do "miraculous" things through his disciples. That means you and I—anyone who
has enough faith to put the principles into practice—could perform
the same miracles that Jesus shared with us. With this thought, we are
reminded of just how much we do not know.

Current scientific thought supports the limited nature of our present vision. Quantum mechanics is discovering that there is a "spiritual"
realm within the cosmos. We say "spiritual" because that is the realm
of the invisible and nonexperiential. Scientists are discovering a world
of extra dimensions where the laws of space and time no longer apply,
a supernatural world, a world in which anything is possible. The biblical words are being proven, "Nothing is impossible" (Luke 1:37).

The healing power of the human being is immense. Jesus tapped
into this divine power, and the physical reality was that people became
well. By reading these pages, you can discover the power to find health,
wholeness, and peace. It can become your own personal miracle.

Read this book and allow it to change the way you think and feel. Give it to a friend. Our hope is that everyone will realize that the power of Possibility Living can add years to their life and life to their years with God's health plan.

Before you embark, however, take the following quiz. Not only does it offer insight into how effective or ineffective your current habits are, but it will also help you to realize how you can best achieve the fullest possible life. The time is now.

ARE YOU REACHING YOUR GOD-GIVEN POTENTIAL?

This easy-to-take quiz will help you discover how effectively you are experiencing God's plan of *Possibility Living*. The higher your score, the closer you are to living to your fullest God-given potential.

Circle the number next to each statement that best describes your habits. Then total your circled numbers for each section.

Ratings

0 – Never or Not at All
1 – Rarely
2 – Seldom
3 – Sometimes
4 – Usually or Most of the Time
5 – Always

General Health

0 1 2 3 4 5   I exercise at least three to four days a week for a minimum of twenty minutes daily.

0 1 2 3 4 5   I maintain an ideal body weight for my age and size.

0 1 2 3 4 5   I rely on traditional medical care for emergency and crisis treatment, yet I maintain

my good health with dietary supplements, chiropractic visits, good nutrition, and exercise.

0 1 2 3 4 5   I do not take prescription drugs for any ongoing physical condition.

_____   TOTAL FOR THIS SECTION

Lifestyle

0 1 2 3 4 5   I abstain from the use of tobacco and limit my alcohol intake to no more than one glass of wine a day.

0 1 2 3 4 5   I have a positive mental outlook and believe that I can live a vital, energized life to the age of 100.

0 1 2 3 4 5   I am calm and peaceful inside and out. I do not worry or become agitated and upset when problems arise.

0 1 2 3 4 5   I get at least seven hours of sleep each night.

_____   TOTAL FOR THIS SECTION

Dietary and Nutritional Habits

0 1 2 3 4 5   I eat at least two servings of green leafy vegetables a day.

0 1 2 3 4 5   I avoid eating fried foods, processed foods, or foods high in fat.

0 1 2 3 4 5   I abstain from consuming white sugar and white flour.

0 1 2 3 4 5   I read the labels when I shop and buy only healthy and chemical-free foods.

_____   TOTAL FOR THIS SECTION

Spirituality

0 1 2 3 4 5   I visit a place of worship at least twice a month.

0 1 2 3 4 5   I have a personal relationship with God and positive relationships with my family, spiritual leaders, and friends.

0 1 2 3 4 5   I give back to the community through volunteer and outreach work or through donations.

0 1 2 3 4 5   I have a daily quiet time when I pray, read Scripture, meditate, or reflect.

_____   TOTAL FOR THIS SECTION

Stress and Work

0 1 2 3 4 5   I respond positively to stress instead of reacting negatively with feelings of hopelessness.

0 1 2 3 4 5   I do not bury my emotions; instead, I constructively release feelings such as joy, love, anger, and concern.

0 1 2 3 4 5   I have (or had) a positive relationship with my parent(s) and/or guardians.

0 1 2 3 4 5   I feel that my work is a gift or calling from God that is part of my destiny, not just a job or drudgery to be endured.

_____   TOTAL FOR THIS SECTION

Computing Your Score

_____   Total points for General Health

_____   Total points for Lifestyle

_____   Total points for Dietary and Nutritional Habits

_____   Total points for Spirituality

_____   Total points for Stress and Work

_____   GRAND TOTAL (Add all of the above points together.)

Interpreting Your Score

99 to 100   Retake the test, and this time be honest. If you are convinced you were honest, read *Possibility Living* and learn to lighten up! Healthy and happy living is not about restrictions, but about enjoying life.

80 to 98   Congratulations. You are on the path to *Possibility Living*. Read this book to refuel and stay on course.

60 to 79   Better than average, but you need continued motivation and additional information to maintain wellness and to grow into *Possibility Living*. This book will enable you to fine-tune your life so that you can reach your full potential.

40 to 59   In need of some help and motivation. Your life's journey is going fairly well, but you are settling for the status quo and missing the mark on enjoying *Possibility Living*. Don't be afraid to read on and make the change to total wellness for your body, mind, and spirit.

20 to 39   Ouch! You are experiencing pain and limitations that will sabotage the benefits of *Possibility Living*. Read and discover how to make significant corrections to reverse the damage caused by toxins, bad habits, and negative attitudes.

0 to 19   Alert! You are living far below your God-given potential. Read *Possibility Living* as soon as possible and challenge yourself to turn negatives into positives.

Whatever your score, *Possibility Living* is for you! Begin with at least one area (perhaps with the section with the lowest score) and add years to your life and life to your years!

Give yourself the gift of *Possibility Living* in all its abundance. Remember that God loves you and has a good plan and purpose for your life.

CHAPTER 1

POSSIBILITY LIVING BY FAITH

Dr. Robert A. Schuller

Faith forms the foundation of Possibility Living. Without it we go nowhere and do nothing. Now, I am referring to faith as a verb, not as a noun. Faith as a noun puts life in a box. As a noun, faith becomes divisive and argumentative. It says, "I am a Catholic," "I am a Buddhist," "I am a Mormon," or "I am a Protestant." And then we start to ask the question, "What faith are you?" If that question were asked of a random group of individuals, there would be almost as many answers as there are people in the room. Some would answer "Baptist," while others might call themselves "Muslim" or "atheist."

Faith as a verb, however, energizes life. It affirms, "I am living a life filled and overflowing with possibilities." The faith to which I refer speaks about a lifestyle, not a creed; a way of life, not a religion. Faith defined by the author of Hebrews becomes the fabric of Possibility Living: "Now faith is the substance of things hoped for, the evidence of things not seen" (Heb. 11:1).

My dear late friend Dr. Norman Vincent Peale directed us to focus on Positive Thinking. His influence on me was so great that it's impossible for me to hear or use the word "positive" or any derivative of it without thinking of him. His book *The Power of Positive Thinking* was one of the most influential books of all time. Reintegrating psychology and religion, Peale developed a cognitive approach to retraining the brain to think positive thoughts. By merging positive thinking with Christian beliefs, he was successful in changing countless lives.

Faith originates in the mind. Cognitively we talk ourselves into seeing the positive in the negative and that begins the process of Positive Thinking. Through Positive Thinking, we can see whatever happens in the present from an optimistic perspective.

Dr. Robert H. Schuller gave us the next step with Possibility Thinking. He put a handle on Positive Thinking by helping people to not only think positive thoughts and find hope, but also see the possibilities in making things happen. This helps individuals turn their dreams into reality. In Possibility Thinking, we can see our future from a positive perspective—filled and brimming over with possibilities.

Possibility Living now completes the circle by helping us put our thoughts, dreams, and hopes into action by living them. Possibility Living uses faith to take the positive steps necessary to transform thinking and possibilities into action—a healthy lifestyle in all aspects of body, mind, and spirit. In Possibility Living, we integrate Positive Thinking and Possibility Thinking into a way of life.

In hope are planted the seeds of faith. Before we can grow faith, we must have the soil of hope. Positive Thinking originates and produces the soil of hope. Faith springs out of the hope. Without hope, nothing exists but despair and oppression. We can begin to break out of hopelessness and into optimism using Positive and Possibility Thinking, and then through faith we initiate the process of Possibility Living. We start with hope, move into faith, make right choices, and then begin living out life's abundant possibilities. I have had difficulty in the past differentiating between faith and hope. Then I discovered this reality—hope is the first step to faith. Out of the soil of hope generated through Possibility Thinking comes a faith that activates Possibility Living.

Hope helps us take the first step of beginning to live, because without hope life is not worth living. But hope goes far beyond wishful thinking. Wishful thinking often drifts aimlessly in fantasy, but hope springs out of reality and truth. Out of living hope grows a faith that produces life! Scripture tells us that God in his mercy has given us new birth into a living hope (1 Pet. 1:3). From this living hope grows a vital, dynamic faith that translates our thoughts into actual planning and strategizing and then into positive, Possibility Thinking.

Positive Thinking says, "I can respond positively to life's situations." Possibility Thinking takes it a step further saying, "Maybe there is a way. Maybe it is possible to overcome the impossible." And thus, hope is born.

Once born anew, living hope begins to think the positive thoughts through which we, by faith, can take action. Possibility Thinking begins the process of actually solving the problem. We ask ourselves, "What are some of the possibilities that could take place to resolve my problems?" The positive thoughts, the "maybes," become the possibility thoughts, "I can. There is a way. It's possible!" Possibility Living by hope and faith steps out of the realm of thinking into the reality of living. We actually live the possibilities!

Living the possibilities is a critical step in actualizing God's dream and desire for your life. When my father, Robert H. Schuller, started his ministry in Garden Grove, California, in 1954, he had no place to have worship services. This was a serious problem, because the Reformed Church in America had hired him to start a new church. If he had not been a positive thinker, he would have packed his bags and moved to an established church somewhere else. Instead of packing his bags and quitting, he made a list of ten places where it might be possible to hold services. Without knowing what it was called, he was practicing Possibility Thinking. His list included the local schools, Seventh-Day Adventist churches (which hold worship on Saturdays), a mortuary, a synagogue, and a drive-in movie theater. As it turned out, the only place available to him was the drive-in theater, and so he started what is today the Crystal Cathedral.

When my father started working his plan—putting possibility thoughts into action—he stepped into Possibility Living. Out of his lifestyle of Possibility Living developed a ministry with a worldwide telecast reaching literally millions every Sunday.

Possibility Living integrates Positive Thinking with Possibility Thinking and then acts! A beautiful example of how this process works can be seen in the expansion of the many freeways in California since 1995. The road crews perform incredible engineering feats in making improvements, including construction of the immense bridges linking the freeways together, around six flowing lanes of high-speed traffic.

My twelve-year-old son was watching as the scaffolding went up piece by piece and as the bridges began to take shape. One day as Anthony watched the builders he exclaimed to his mother, "How in the world do these men know how to build these bridges?"

My wife, Donna, in her wonderful wisdom, turned to Anthony and said, "Anthony, it's just like building with your Legos. The builders have plans and instructions, and they start with the first two pieces in step one. When they put those two pieces together, they go to step two and they assemble those pieces together. On they go to step three. Then step four. They just follow the plans until they reach the end. That's how they build those wonderful bridges."

And Anthony replied, "Oh, of course!"

Positive Thinking says there must be a way to handle all the traffic and still get the work done. Possibility Thinking makes the plans to accommodate the traffic and the work. Possibility Living takes the next step in the series and starts building the freeways, i.e., living the possibilities. Plans will be of no use unless we put them to practice. Faith integrates Positive Thinking and Possibility Thinking to the point where we can act through faith and hope—that's Possibility Living.

I've been taught that by beginning you are already half done. If you can just get started, you're halfway there. That is where faith or Possibility Living, is born. When you take the first step, you realize that "possibly it can be done."

The man who misses all the fun
*   is he who says, "It can't be done."*
In solemn pride he stands aloof
*   and greets each venture with reproof.*
Had he the power, he'd efface
*   the history of the human race.*
We would have no radio. No motorcars.
*   No street lit by electric stars.*

No telegraph or telephone.
   We'd linger in the age of stone.
The world would sleep if things were run
   By men who say, "It can't be done."

                    Anonymous

Though blind and deaf, Helen Keller said, "I am only one, but still I am one. I cannot do everything, but still I can do something. I will not refuse to do the something I can do." Possibility Living is taking the action to make the Positive Thinking and the Possibility Thinking work. The combination of all three is what I call faith—the substance of things hoped for and the evidence of things not yet seen. Substance and evidence speak of concrete action that has transformed thoughts into lived-out possibilities.

POSSIBILITY LIVING: BODY, MIND, AND SPIRIT

When we integrate Possibility Living into every area of life, we see that it works just as well with the physical as it does with the mental and the spiritual. Relating Possibility Living to our health and wellness, we realize that we can add years to our life and life to those years. "Maybe I don't have to slowly disintegrate as I age. Maybe the Bible holds true when it reveals that I can live up to 120 years and that, like Moses, I can be healthy until the day I die." That is Positive Thinking. "If this is true what plans can I make to see it happen? What foods should I eat and thoughts should I think to make that happen?" This is the birth of Possibility Thinking. In this book we offer you many tools, truths, and practical insights to help you start your journey to health and wholeness and thus move into Possibility Living. The next step is up to you. What actions are you going to take so that you can begin to experience a whole faith combining body, mind, and spirit?

Possibility Living integrates health sciences with our faith, giving us the spiritual (Positive Thinking), the mental (Possibility Thinking), and the physical manifestation (Possibility Living) to incorporate the wholeness of body, mind, and spirit. What good will it do us if we have the positive thoughts and we start moving toward the possibilities, only to have our bodies fail us? Without the integration of health science into our faith, we run the risk of failure. Not because of a lack of motivation or negative thinking, but simply because our bodies won't have the strength to carry us through. The harder you push your body, the more attention you will need to give to making the right choices.

I discovered the truth of how bad choices can interrupt Possibility Living while writing this book. In order to meet the deadlines for publication while maintaining my work schedule, I decided that I would wake up at 4:00 A.M. every morning to write. This would give me nearly four hours of uninterrupted time every day. This worked very well and I was able to accomplish my goal. But in the process of pushing my body, I also made some bad choices about what to eat. It was during the holidays and sweets were at my desk constantly. I enjoyed the season and vowed to rectify my behavior after the book was completed. I also forgot to take my vitamins for two days straight. Not only was I pushing my body, I was also poisoning it and not even giving it adequate nourishment with which to function.

In my arrogance, I assumed that my body and my immune system would be able to withstand the punishment I was giving them. I was wrong. On New Year's Eve, I got the flu and found myself in bed with a fever and all the other symptoms that go along with that illness. If I had it to do over again, I would have taken my vitamins and pushed away some of the treats. This would have given my body the nourishment it needed to fight off the virus. But even though I did get sick, because I had a history of wellness care and immediately did everything to promote health, I recovered in a matter of days instead of weeks. But I learned again that although our bodies can take tremendous punishment for extended periods of time, we need to give them the nourishment they need to act upon all the possibilities we have planned in life.

When you tax your body greatly with extra hours of stress and the poisons of sugar and other nonfoods and give it no nourishment, don't expect to sail through without paying a price. For me, the price was several uncomfortable days with the flu. If I had ignored the message my body gave me, ingested different medications just to get rid of the symptoms, and kept up that kind of pace and eating habits, I could expect to pay a much higher price in the future—like heart failure, cancer, stroke, diabetes, or a host of other serious illnesses.

MY HEALTH AND POSSIBILITY LIVING

Later in this book, my friend and coauthor, Dr. Douglas Di Siena, will share with you some of his story. But I want to take a moment to share with you how I began taking my first steps into using Possibility Living to experience greater health. I have the privilege of hosting a radio program, which I have been doing since 1995. When we started the radio program, it was live, and whenever we had someone on talking about health and nutrition, the phones rang nonstop. Everyone seemed to be interested in the subject of eating right and staying healthy.

So I kept inviting more and more health and nutrition people to be on the radio show. This has provided me with a great education and enormous insight. On a regular basis, I talk to some of the finest, cutting-edge people in the field health and wellness, the people writing the current groundbreaking books and articles. As a result, I've been able to stay current with the latest developments in this field. On the show I can ask people any questions I want. I've got their attention for thirty minutes, so I just gather priceless information.

I became interested in health, however, long before I started the radio program. In the early 1980s I had a physical and learned from my physician that my cholesterol was a little high. I wasn't overly concerned. Actually, I thought it was just a fluke and not an accurate test. When I went back to see him again, my doctor said we should watch my cholesterol level closely.

At the physical, my cholesterol was 200. A few weeks later it was tested again. It had shot up to 218. It had started out borderline and now it was flying up into the danger zone. It was going the wrong way and moving fast! My doctor advised me to cut eggs out of my diet; so I did. But what really caught my attention was that, for the first time in my life, I had something concrete that said I was not in perfect health. And I was only in my early thirties. I thought, "I'm too young to have cholesterol problems. I don't want to have a heart attack when I'm fifty years old."

So I started studying cholesterol. At the time, the best-selling book on cholesterol was by Kenneth Cooper, *Controlling Your Cholesterol.* I bought that book and devoured it, studying it like a textbook.

That bout with high cholesterol began my education in nutrition. I soon realized that there is a lot to our diet that we need to be aware of and it's not simply cutting out eggs. Cutting out eggs is not enough to control cholesterol.

In facing my high cholesterol, I concluded that I had three different choices when it comes to food: fats, carbohydrates, and proteins. All food can be put into one of these three categories. There is much debate today about what percentages of each we need in our diet. We will discuss this later, but for the sake of my testimony, I thought my solution was to cut the fat. "You are what you eat" was the slogan that ran through my head. I came to that conclusion through my friend Jim Kubicka. He was on a "no fat" diet. For instance, he would order a salad and for dressing just vinegar. I asked him why and he said, "Salad oils and dressings are very high fat and I'm avoiding all fats."

I had no idea what foods contained fats or what fats even were. So I bought a book called *The 22 Gram Solution,* by Corrine T. Netzer. It basically shows you what foods contain fat and how much fat they have. I started living "fat free," which is not eating any fats at all. I would basically eat just carbohydrates with some lean protein from meat. It worked very well as far as my cholesterol was concerned. I had another cholesterol test a few months later and it was below 150.

Since then, I have learned that it is more important to eat the right kind of fats than to watch the amount of fat. There are good fats and bad fats. You can eat good fats, enjoy them, and your body will like them. The good fats are the fats that come from God's food! God's foods are natural, unprocessed whole foods. God's food has good fats like the fats in fish, olives, and avocados. Fats begin to turn against us only when we begin to manipulate them. Simple cooking begins to change the structure of the fat. By the time we molecularly change the fat by adding hydrogen molecules (hydrogenated fat), fat becomes an enemy of the body.

Later, in Chapter 6, Doug will share with you in more detail how to eat right and take care of your body. For now, I simply want to emphasize that the sooner we start caring for our bodies, the sooner Possibility Living begins to positively impact our lives. Positive Thinking, Possibility Thinking, and Possibility Living all depend on a healthy body to make it possible to translate hope and faith into action.

God gave us these incredible vehicles, our bodies, to carry us through life. If we care for our bodies, they will care for us. This book will give you many truths to help you in this endeavor. We can be confident we will enjoy the promises of a long, healthy, and happy life if we continue to make the right choices. We can live free from the worry of cancer, stroke, heart failure, diabetes and all of the other problems that plague our society when we practice Possibility Living.

PRAYER WITHOUT FAITH IS DEAD

In addition to caring for our bodies, we must also care for our mind and spirit. Positive Thinking begins with prayer. It is here that we are changed from negative to positive thinkers. Dr. Norman Vincent Peale said it this way: "Prayer doesn't always change things for you, but it does change you for things." We will talk about prayer throughout this book because without it there is no hope, and without hope there is nothing.

If you ever travel to Rome, one thing you absolutely must see is the Sistine Chapel at St. Peter's Basilica. The Sistine Chapel, painted by Michelangelo, is one of the most phenomenal pieces of art in history. On the ceiling of the chapel is Michelangelo's famous painting of God's finger reaching down to touch Adam, who is reaching his finger up to touch God.

When I think of prayer, that is what I think of—reaching out to touch God. We are reaching out to feel who God is. We are reaching out to understand the purpose and course God wants us to take. That's my understanding of prayer.

But if all we ever do is connect with God in prayer and never start down our path of Possibility Living, then our prayers are nothing more than chanting canticles and vain repetitions. We become so heavenly minded that we become no earthly good. We can pray without works, but our prayers are for nothing until they work on us. We need power behind our prayers and that comes from moving our hope by faith into possibilities. Our prayers must be powered with faith, because prayer without faith is dead.

A few years ago I went to Hershey, Pennsylvania, to deliver a message at a prayer breakfast. I was able to take my entire family along by using my accumulated airline miles. When we arrived in Hershey, we could smell the chocolate aroma that penetrates the air of that beautiful town. Wow, did the children ever get excited. They couldn't wait to see the chocolate factory. They grew up watching the movie *Willy Wonka and the Chocolate Factory*, so they had all kinds of chocolate-factory images bouncing through their minds. Then they saw the Hershey Amusement Park. In the middle of that park is a roller coaster named "The Wildcat." We had arrived at night, and there was a string of lights going around the entire track so you could see every turn, spin, corner dive, and hill that the roller coaster makes as it zips its way around the track.

When my children saw the lights flashing wildly, they got so excited they were jumping up and down in the backseat of the car shouting, "Can we go on the Wildcat, Dad? Can we go on the Wildcat, please?"

Greg, our escort, rescued me saying, "Gee, I'm sorry kids. The park is closed these days."

And I murmured in gratitude, "Thank you, Lord."

That night as we tucked the children into bed, I heard them pray, "Dear God, help us to be able to go on the Wildcat."

Now what am I going to do? There's no way they will be able to go on the Wildcat.

Early the next morning Greg Anderson telephoned, "Guess who is going to be at our prayer breakfast this morning?"

I said, "Who?"

"The general manager of the Hershey Amusement Park and he said he would open the park just for your family!" And he did.

He met us in the parking lot and walked us to the Wildcat roller coaster, where the maintenance men were waiting for us. We rode in the front seats, then the backseats, and then the middle. Around and around the track we went, spinning and turning, up and down, over and under all the hills. What a ride. We must have gone through the course ten times. It was wonderful.

My children learned the power of prayer that day, and they learned that prayer with faith performs miracles. As we pray we look for the blessing that God will send our way. Be ready to move when he says go. When God says go, put on your track shoes.

FAITH WITHOUT WORKS IS DEAD

Without putting faith into action, faith quickly becomes that static noun "religion." The process is one of the great deceptions that take place on a spiritual level. If we cannot be led into overt sinful behavior, maybe we can be led into the sin of sloth. Classic theology uses the terms "sin by commission" and "sin by omission."

Sin by commission is what most people think of when they think of sin—the direct negative actions that violate the laws of God and cause so much pain in people's lives. It is intentional disobedience to God and his will for your life.

Sin by omission is much more subtle. It is the sin of doing nothing. If you see someone in dire need and you have the ability to help but turn and walk the other way—that is a sin of omission. If we think about our sins of omission, we become extremely humble before God because we realize that throughout life we could always have done more.

The award-winning historical movie *Schindler's List*, directed by Steven Spielberg, has a very dramatic and touching conclusion. I cry every time I see it. The movie depicts the horror of the Jewish plight during World War II. Schindler is a German businessman who sees the opportunity of financial profit from Jewish labor. He takes full advantage of the political environment and becomes very wealthy off the "slave labor." As the Nazi atrocities increase, Schindler becomes sympathetic to the Jews and allies himself with them, saving many from the death camps. As the movie concludes, Schindler spends his entire fortune to "buy" Jews for his factory labor force.

In the closing scene, which brings tears to my eyes, he looks at over one thousand men, women, and children he has saved and then breaks down in tears, weeping because he could have done more. He is ready to drive away in his car and through his tears he cries out, "This car, I could have saved twenty people with her. This ring, I could have saved two more. This watch, one more. I could have done more. I could have done more." Finally he falls to the ground in sorrow for all he could have done and didn't do.

I once heard that hell is seeing everything we could have been or done if we only had acted on our faith. This is the sin of omission. It is the failure to trust God and to move out in faith and do what he has called us to do. But remember that no matter how much you do, it will never be enough. That is why we need the grace of Jesus Christ to carry us through. Because of him we do our best, and when we fail he carries us the rest of the way.

The question is: "Do you have a faith without works or are you putting your faith into action?" Faith without works is dead. As you set about doing the will of God and fulfilling your calling and destiny, remember the words of Nike, the athletic shoe manufacturer, "Just do it!" So get moving and put your faith to work.

WORKS WITHOUT LOVE ARE DEAD

The end does not justify the means. We must live a life of love if we are going to live at all. "There is faith, hope and love, and the greatest of these is love." So wrote the apostle Paul in that classic scripture 1 Corinthians 13. That passage has transcended the walls of religion to break into the core of our humanity and spirituality. A dear friend of mine, a Jewish rabbi, was celebrating his son's bar mitzvah. During the service, he turned to me and said, "Please do not reveal the source of this reading," and then proceeded to read the "love chapter" from Corinthians. Love is essential to life's possibilities. The Bible says that

God is love. To live without love leads to life's greatest tragedy and travesty—life without God.

We have talked about sins of commission and omission, but all sin, at its foundation, is separation from God. The Good News announces that Jesus forgives all sin. He is the bridge. He fills the gap between God and us. He fills our "God-shaped void" (Pascel) with love and brings us back to God.

Billy was sitting in his elementary classroom. About five minutes before recess, he really had to go to the bathroom. Ignoring the teacher, all he could do was count down the seconds until break. He intently watched the second hand on the clock as it plodded endlessly around going nowhere. Time seemed to be standing still. Suddenly the teacher called his name. Totally unprepared and startled, he wet his pants.

When Billy didn't answer, the teacher asked the next student. No one realized that Billy had a puddle around his feet. His shoes and socks were dripping wet. Now he was worried about how to get out of the room without the other kids noticing what had happened. What was he going to do now? Soon the bell would ring. He would have to stand up, and everyone would see his wet pants. Then he would be ridiculed. He would be so ashamed. So he sat there completely humiliated and mortified by the thought of what would take place in the next sixty seconds.

With his pants wet and a puddle at his feet, he was faced with the only thing he knew to do in a situation like this. He prayed. "Dear God, please help me out of this mess. Please, please, please." When he opened his eyes, there was Sarah, walking right toward him carrying her goldfish bowl. Just before she reached him, she tripped and the water poured all over him. He jumped out of his chair scolding Sarah. Billy yelled out, "How dare you spill all that water on me!" but inside he was whispering, "Thank you, Jesus! Thank you, God!"

Sarah was in trouble now, and Billy became the object of sympathy. Poor Billy. Poor little guy—Sarah really got him wet. All the way down to his shoes. While he went to change into his gym clothes and get cleaned up, all the rest of the kids helped Sarah clean up the mess. Sarah became the object of scorn and ridicule.

Everyone sympathized with Billy that day and gave him a lot of extra love, so the rest of his day went really well for him. By the end of the day Sarah was sitting all by herself, waiting for the bus. Billy strolled over to Sarah wearing his gym clothes and carrying his bag of wet clothes over his shoulder. When no one was looking, he moved over to her and said, "Sarah, you did that on purpose, didn't you?"

Sarah said, "Yes, Billy. I wet my pants once too."

Works without love are dead. You can build the greatest empires the world has ever seen, but if you lack love, it profits you nothing. You can change the course of history, but if you have not love, work fades into oblivion. "The greatest of these is love."

FAITH—USE IT OR LOSE IT

Faith is like a muscle—the more you use it, the stronger it becomes. If you never use it, it atrophies and dies. As with exercise, you need to start easy and grow into the more challenging. Start small and think tall. Start with something that will build confidence and assurance. You can see how this dynamic works with the example of an exercise program. Begin by taking a ten-minute stroll. Commit to a brisk walk six days a week. Take Sundays off and rest. It is the day you set aside each week to prepare spiritually for the challenges of the upcoming week. If the six days of walking went well, extend your time or distance.

If you continue to do this for a year or two, you will be able run or walk a marathon! I wouldn't recommend that you actually run marathons, because they are so hard on your body, but to have a body capable of completing a marathon is an admirable goal. You can have that ability if you work at it one step at a time. You can make every excuse imaginable for why you can't do it, which is classic negative thinking. You can look at your current health or age and assume that it would be impossible for you. But faith says, "I can overcome the obstacles."

One of the great faith stories of all time is the biblical event in which Joshua crosses the Jordan River to accept the land promised by God. It required tremendous trust in God, who had led the Israelites through the wilderness for the past forty years. The story really begins twenty years earlier when Moses, at the spry age of one hundred, led his people to the edge of the same river after freeing them from Pharaoh and wandering with them for twenty years. During the first twenty years, God displayed his power in numerous ways and continued to tell Moses about the promised land he would give to him and his people.

So the time came for Moses to enter the land flowing with milk and honey. The first thing he did was to send ten spies into the land to measure the opposition. The spies came back with news of giant men and impenetrable walls. Not good news for Moses and the Israelites. Of the ten spies, two thought that with God all things were possible and that they should continue the campaign. Those two were Joshua and Caleb. The other eight thought that it would be suicide. Moses decided that he would rather wander in the wilderness the rest of his life than take a chance with God, so he turned back and spent the rest of his life wandering.

Now, twenty years later, God has led Moses and his people back to the edge of the same river. As I mentioned earlier, Moses died at the age of 120, strong and with good eyes, but he never entered the land that God offered him because, when the opportunity presented itself, Moses lost his faith and wouldn't follow. He practiced Positive Thinking and Possibility Thinking, but he did not use Possibility Living in this circumstance.

With the death of Moses, Joshua is given the challenge to lead God's people into the promised land. Now he stands and looks at the land he saw with his own eyes twenty years earlier. Of the ten spies only he and Caleb are living. All the naysayers have died (biblical proof that Positive Thinking adds years to your life). Then God says to Joshua:

Moses my servant is dead. Now then, you and all these people get ready to cross the Jordan River into the land I am about to give to them—the Israelites. I will give you every place where you set your foot as I promised Moses. . . . No one will be able to stand up against you all the days of your life. As I was with Moses, so I will be with you: I will never leave you nor forsake you. Be strong and courageous, because you will lead these people to inherit the land I swore to their forefathers to give them. Be strong and very courageous. Be careful to obey all the laws my servant Moses gave you, do not turn from it to the right or to the left, that you may be successful wherever you go. Do not let this Book of the Law depart from your mouth; meditate on it day and night, so that you may be careful to do everything written in it. Then you will be prosperous and successful. Have I not commanded you? Be strong and courageous. Do not be terrified: do not be discouraged, for the Lord your God will be with you wherever you go.

Joshua 1:2–9

I believe that the words God spoke to Joshua are given to millions of people throughout history and are given to you. The only thing that stands between our promised land and us is making a right choice in courage and faith to follow God's will for our lives. God told Joshua three times, "Be strong and very courageous." That is the message he wants us to hear. Possibility Living steps up to the "river," or line, with positive thoughts filled with possibilities and then acts by faith to cross it. That is a significant step to wholeness. I believe that God is referring to every part of us — body, mind, and spirit — when he gives us the command to be strong and act on our faith in his promise.

Body, mind, and spirit are one. You cannot improve one without helping the others. You cannot damage one without hurting the others. You can start with your body, mind, or spirit and the others will follow. It is like personal awareness and understanding God: when you come to know more about yourself, you will come to know more about God. The opposite is also true. When you seek to know more about God, you will come to know more about yourself.

As we will discover throughout this book, traditional medicine has attempted to mechanize the body and treat it as though it were disconnected from the whole, like a machine, as if the spiritual and the physical were separate. Today, modern health care is realizing the need to care for the whole person and discovering the tremendous benefits of supporting life instead of fighting disease. There is tremendous danger in fighting disease, because in that process, we fight life. I am a firm believer that God created a strong human body that can naturally fight off incredible numbers of bacteria and viruses to maintain health as long as we nourish it, detoxify it, and protect it from injury. I propose that a large percentage of deaths come from three sources: *toxins* (poisons), *lack of nourishment,* and *injury.*

1. *Toxins.* In order to picture the way toxins attack the body on a regular basis, I ask people to imagine a barrel hanging on a chain. The chain is your DNA, or gene code. The barrel is your body. From the moment of birth, your barrel begins to fill with toxins. It starts with the neurotoxins caused by the trauma of a forced delivery and continues when you receive inoculations laced with mercury and other toxins used to kill live polio or other viruses. You may go to a home environment filled with smoke, pesticides, preservatives, and chemicals that God never intended for human consumption. The barrel begins to fill.

   Added to the obvious toxins are the not so obvious and often more dangerous toxins that come from negative thinking, stress, negative habits, relationships, finances, religion, and physiology. But the human body is so resilient that it keeps on going without missing a beat. The body struggles to continue until the barrel becomes so heavy with toxic waste that a weak link in the DNA chain eventually breaks, usually in a person's later years. Which link breaks depends on family history, and the result is cancer, arthritis, heart ailments, diabetes, or other disease.

   Disintegrating health is due more to a toxic lifestyle than anything else. But there is a way to empty your barrel, relieve the pressure upon the DNA chain, and live a full abundant life! In the following pages you will discover the things you can do to give your body the full expression of life, or ability to function in an optimal way, that it deserves. We will empower you with the knowledge to make the choices you need to experience not only longer life, but a life filled with living out your God-given possibilities.

2. *Lack of Nourishment.* We will show you how to nourish your body so that it will have the fuel it needs to perform like a well-tuned race car. Homeostasis is the state of balance required for the body to operate at full capacity. Blood tests can quickly determine the nutrients your body is lacking. The chemicals that are out of alignment tell the story of lack of exercise, poor eating choices, and toxic lifestyle. With the aid of a well-trained professional, you can determine a course of action you will need to take to achieve a balanced body.

   We will talk about some essentials, however, that every body needs. Because of the overprocessed food that has infiltrated most American diets today, we must supplement our diets with some basic vitamins and minerals to prevent premature aging and oxidation of organ tissue.

3. *Injury.* Injuries take the lives of thousands of people every year. They can happen anytime and anywhere. There are no guarantees in life. That is why we must recognize the gift of life every day and thank God for allowing us the privilege of living yet another day. The most difficult funerals for me have been those of teens. Unfortunately, I have had several. One died in a dentist's chair. Many have died in automobile accidents. They are all difficult. But every time I have a funeral of someone who has died suddenly from some form of injury, it reminds me that life truly is a gift and to thank God every day for his generosity.

Remember that death is not the end of life, but a new beginning. It is not termination, but transition. When we have faith in Christ, death is simply stepping over the line from mortality into eternal life. We cannot escape death, but we don't have to get there prematurely. We want you to finish strong like Moses. Our prayer is that death comes only after you have fulfilled the calling God has given you.

In Possibility Living, you will discover how to

- be vital up to 100 years of age

- make the right choices for living a long and full life

- live *Above, Down, Inside,* and *Out*

- choose a healthy diet and fit lifestyle

- detoxify your relationships, thoughts, stress, habits, foods, finances, words, religion, physiology, and environment

- release the power of Possibility Living through faith and God's power

The purpose of this book is to give you the knowledge to make the right decisions to experience a full, healthy, and complete life, living to the very end. Cross your Jordan today and experience the promised land that God has given you. "Be strong and very courageous." Possibility Living can become a reality for you!

CHAPTER 2

POSSIBILITY LIVING FOR A VITAL 100

Dr. Douglas Di Siena

Picture a burning candle. A candle's light begins with a spark and then burns brightly and continuously with the same force and power until its wax is gone. Then with just a gentle flicker, the wick extinguishes and the light gracefully goes out.

A vital flame of Possibility Living resides in all of us, touching every aspect of our being—body, mind, and spirit. Empowered by our creator, we can choose to live to be a vigorous 100 years old with the possibility of reaching 120 just as Moses did in Scripture. "And Moses was one hundred and twenty years old when he died: his eye was not dim, nor his natural force abated" (Deut. 34:7). That we could live to be 120 years old might seem so incredulous that you would sigh, "I never want to get that old." But Moses was just as alive at 120 as he was as a young man. Scripture asserts the remarkable truth—his eyes were not dim, nor his natural force abated. How is it possible for you to live to be a vital 100 or older? Though your past may have been filled with limiting, even toxic, habits, thoughts, attitudes, and behaviors, you can begin Possibility Living today.

My patients often regret that they have not lived their lives to the fullest extent and made use of all the possibilities available to them.

Some wistfully wish they could return to their twenties and start over again. Perhaps you feel that way. But it is never too late to begin living your life filled with right choices that will maintain your physical, mental, emotional, and spiritual health.

In Possibility Living, there is no room for the paradigm of degeneration, chronic sickness, and all of the painful, debilitating diseases that have become an acceptable part of aging. Over the years I have seen so many people with a preventable condition called *coxim malum senilis*, meaning "an old, bad hip." In other words, one hip is in constant pain. When I ask patients how that hip reached such a condition, they explain, "It's just my age." My response, tongue in cheek, is always, "How old is your other hip?"

If one hip had degenerated solely due to age, then it would seem to me that the other hip should be equally degenerated. Once we accept the idea that it is not normal to suffer from "age-related" disorders, we can then be empowered by a new sense of optimism. We can be victorious over most afflictions once we take responsibility for where we are and where we are going with our health.

The dental profession began their educational process with my generation while we were impressionable young children. I can remember dentists coming to our classrooms and explaining how we could have healthy teeth and gums that would last a lifetime. They told us that teeth were made to last over the course of our entire lives. Therefore, we should not wait for a toothache to see the dentist. Instead, we should have our teeth cleaned regularly. And to keep our teeth and gums healthy, we must not merely rely solely on dentists. Instead, we must take care of ourselves by brushing, flossing, and staying away from environmental toxins like sugar. In short, our dentists gave us a vision and a new paradigm for keeping all of our teeth healthy for life.

MAINTAINING HEALTH RATHER THAN TREATING DISEASE

Each of us has a philosophy of health and healing. This philosophy is created by our paradigms—the way we view the world and our life experiences. As a result of our paradigms, we choose to behave in certain ways. These behaviors, when repeated over a relatively brief time, often result in very predictable health outcomes. As we begin this wonderful journey toward Possibility Living—health, wholeness, and healing—we must develop an understanding of our present state of health and our paradigms, or thoughts on health, wholeness, and healing. Robert A. Aldrich, M.D., has remarked, "The maintenance of health should take precedence over the treatment of disease."[1] We agree. The choices we make determine our destiny. We can choose Possibility Living over lifestyles that debilitate our health and sabotage our future.

Health issues occupy the thoughts of commentators, laypeople, and health professionals alike, because many in our culture are looking for a better way of life. Increasing numbers of people are seeking more natural means of health care. According to an astounding recent study by D. M. Eisenberg, M.D., the increase in annual visits to alternative practitioners grew from 427 million to 629 million, nearly double the number of visits to all primary-care physicians (386 million). What is more interesting, according to this study, the probability of an alternative care user seeing an alternative practitioner increased from 36.3 percent (22 million people) to 46.3 percent (39 million people).[2]

Why are so many people seeking an alternative to traditional medicine? Their paradigms are shifting. They are moving from caring for their bodies only when they get sick to becoming proactive in maintaining health all the time. In Possibility Living, we want to make healthy decisions today that lead to a healthier future, instead of ignoring our health today and suffering a debilitating future.

MOVING FROM OUTDATED HEALTH-CARE PARADIGMS INTO POSSIBILITY LIVING

To help illustrate our paradigms in regard to health, we can graph on a continuum four different health paradigms. Let's take a quick look at the graph and then define each position along the "expression of life" continuum.

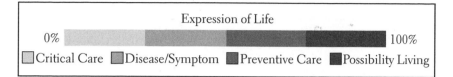

1. *Critical care.* First there are those who find themselves in the critical-care position on the continuum. They presently suffer from a serious or life-threatening illness and are forced to make choices opting only for critical care. It's hard to be proactive about a healthy future when one is battling today just to survive. In the critical-care paradigm, the expression and quality of life are extremely limited. A person is basically in a survival mode.

2. *Disease/symptom care.* Next on the continuum are those caught in the debilitating cycle of trying to treat a chronic disease by addressing only the symptoms. Instead of building up strength and health for a future filled with possibilities, they live in a reactive state spending their energies fighting symptoms so that they can live life on a minimum comfort level. This paradigm is used in traditional medicine. Nothing proactive is done about one's health until disease occurs. Then only the symptoms are treated, while the causes of the disease, which often are rooted in toxic attitudes, stress, habits, foods, and relationships, go unexposed and uneliminated.

   In this paradigm, medical care waits until the patient begins to develop signs or symptoms of illness. Then its primary goal is to treat the disease by reducing or eliminating those signs or symptoms. J. H. Tilden, M.D., observes, "The study of disease per se leads to chaos. Only knowledge of health—the study of health—can give a true knowledge of disease, for disease is handicapped health. Health represents a body and mind adjusted to, and in unison with, the physical laws of nature. And disease represents a departure from this ideal state."[3]

   In the United States, the public spends more money on traditional medical care per capita than in any other industrialized nation on earth. Therefore, we would expect to have the healthiest population on earth—but we don't. Worse yet, we are close to the bottom of the list and getting worse in both infant mortality and life expectancy.

According to the Johns Hopkins School of Public Health, between 1990 and 1995 the United States dropped to 23rd out of the 29 industrialized nations for infant mortality. In 1960, the life expectancy for women was ranked 13th; in 1995 the life expectancy for women dropped to 20th out of 29. Men did even worse. In 1960, men were ranked at 17th; in 1995, we continued to slide down, to 21st place out of 29.[4] Perhaps there could be a better way?

Many of us have experienced the method most doctors use to start their patient care. They ask, "What is your chief complaint?" or more gently, "How do you feel?" Then their primary treatment objective is to remove the feeling or symptom.

Let's use a dental analogy to understand this paradigm. Say you go to a dentist in horrific pain with a puss-filled swollen tooth. Now if the dentist's only concern is treating the pain with a shot of novocaine without giving a thought to the cause of the pain, you would probably be very upset.

Or we might use the illustration of an iceberg. In the movie *Titanic*, the ship sank as a result of hitting an iceberg. The question is: "What is the most dangerous part of an iceberg?" Obviously, it's the part we cannot see. When we remove the symptoms without addressing the cause, we leave behind the dysfunction while removing the body's warning systems.

Traditional health care has created a comfortable way for many to continue along the disease continuum by removing symptoms instead of addressing the real problem or the cause of the symptoms. Think of the traditional model this way:

- The presence of symptoms = disease.

- The absence of symptoms = health.

Too often we are led to believe the false assumption that once our symptoms are eliminated, the disease is cured. This view of health care propagates the idea that prevention should be aimed at the early detection of disease. However, if our goal is simply to detect an illness in its early stages, then the disease has not been prevented. Although this may be a better way to treat disease than delaying treatment until after the disease has significantly progressed to critical care, it does nothing for the promotion of health.

Although we know that removal of symptoms does not create health, we may not be aware that doing so can also be very dangerous. It's interesting to note that this paradigm of treating symptoms is so pervasive that it has even become a health hazard.

Consider this common predicament. Most parents are still taught by their pediatrician to give pain relievers to children to reduce or eliminate the symptom of a fever. Thankfully they have ceased promoting aspirin, which has resulted in countless needless neurological complications. We now know that fevers are not a mistake by God, but rather an important defense mechanism to rid the body of sickness. Elevated body temperature helps to stimulate the immune system, while decreasing the virulence of the germ. I have seen many cases where, if the fever has not abated, an antibiotic was prescribed without a doctor ever seeing the patient. How many antibiotics have been unnecessarily given to children with a runny nose due to viral infection? This is not only ineffective for viral infections, in this case, but it would actually leave the child with an increased susceptibility to further infections.

In my office, we see far too many people in very late stages of spinal degeneration because they have put off dealing with the nerve impingement through self-medication or prescriptions. Certainly, if the red warning light in the instrument panel of your car were flashing, you would know better than to put a piece of black tape over it just to remove the "symptom" or irritation. Procrastination is the thief of health. Eliminating symptoms does not fix any problem or promote health.

However, we understand, appreciate, and applaud those doctors who practice this form of care. When in need of emergency care, I thank God we have a system of highly trained doctors who can administer it. But we let far too many people unnecessarily freefall into this realm of disease, suffering, and despair. People could be much better served armed with information that could not only prevent them from ever having the need to get into crisis care, but also to live a life of full vitality, free from disease and disability. "It is a misnomer to call medicine the healing art. The healing art is the secret wisdom of the body," says Andrew Weil, M.D.[5]

3. *Preventive care.* The third paradigm of care is what most people call prevention. Preventive health care has become very popular lately. This form of care still focuses primarily on symptoms, but treats the symptoms in more natural ways. For example, a fever is still treated as a symptom, as something to be eliminated, but with herbs instead of drugs.

Some people have learned that prevention can lead to an improved expression of life, a life above the mediocrity of merely existing. So they exercise, take vitamins, try to watch what they eat, and usually have a positive outlook on life. Although prevention is certainly a healthier paradigm than the first two, it doesn't reach the quality of life promised in Scripture: "I have come that you might have life and have it more abundantly" (John 10:10).

This type of care still seeks relief from the outside in rather from the inside out. Preventive care still seeks to control the body from *our* perspective, or how we think the body should function, as opposed to how God intended the body to function. Any person altered from the outside will always fall short of God's perfect plan on the inside.

Any treatment, whether it is with drugs or herbs, with the intention to modify function, as opposed to supporting function, still assumes we know more about bodily function than God's creative design within our bodies does. Although this form of care is safer and at times should be used as a necessary alternative, it is still not the way to an optimal expression of life.

Maximum expression of life can only be realized when we

remove all blockages to the expression of this innate created intelligence, whether they are neuroemotional, spiritual, or physical. Whole foods, vitamins, minerals, and herbs are then used to support optimal bodily function, not change it. Therefore our bodies are allowed to function as God has intended. "Mankind has built a gigantic mass of the superiority of the *outside-in* values because he knows little of the superiority of the *above-down inside-out* principle."[6]

4. *Possibility Living.* Living abundantly, with the fullest expression of life, occurs when every aspect of life — body, mind, and spirit — finds full expression daily in physical, emotional, mental, and spiritual well-being.

Keep the "Expression of Life" graph in mind as you consider a paradigm shift from focusing on treating disease to living a life abundantly filled with possibilities. Life's outcomes are ultimately based on choices. You have been given free will — the opportunity to choose the fullest "expression of life" possible.

With free choice comes the responsibility for the outcome. We can choose the victim approach, i.e., waiting until a crisis leaves us no other choice. Victims are usually caught in the stressful state of reacting to one crisis after another. Victims are continuously caught in a critical-care or symptom-care paradigm.

If it takes disease or symptoms of an illness to prompt a change in your choices, then you will remain constantly sick. The best option you have is Possibility Living. Possibility Living involves making right choices about your health before, not just after, you face an illness.

Whenever the author of *Love, Medicine, and Miracles*, oncologist Dr. Bernie Siegel, gave a patient a negative pathological report, he would say, "This means you are on a bad path and now you have a great motivation to change your path." The saddest days in my practice occur when I have to give that type of report, and the patient is left with only a few limited pathways of healing as a result of neglect. Almost all diseases are the result of poor choices and/or the failure to be proactive.

Although there is always hope in every situation, many times the outcome of poor choices results in irreversible negative consequences that can only be overcome miraculously. So before reaching so negative a health state that you require a miracle, why not choose the positive Possibility Living approach to health? Be proactive. You can learn how to make healthy choices that reduce stress and anxiety and take back some control of your life.

No one completely understands the awesome complexity and health possibilities of the human body. However, we do believe that God has created our bodies to operate in a state of health, not disease. Furthermore, the body has in its very structure the Creator's wisdom, which empowers it to stay healthy and overcome almost any outside onslaught from disease.

If we appreciate God's gift of inner healing, then our only task is to remove any blockage that might interfere with this awesome power and its ability to control every cell in our body. Since God placed symptoms in our body for a purpose, we must change our focus in modern health care from treating symptoms to making healthy choices proactively through Possibility Living.

In Possibility Living, we concern ourselves with the source of life, healing, our emotions, and the internal environment. This contrasts to traditional medicine, which typically looks to treat the disease of the person, rather than caring for the person with the disease, and ignoring the larger issues of a person's lifestyle.

This level of "modern health care," or Possibility Living, facilitates the progressive developmental process of the body, mind, and spirit. *Dorland's Medical Dictionary* defines health as "a state of optimal function, physically, emotionally, and socially, not merely the absence of disease or infirmary."[7]

Our quest for the body's optimal function is more than just "getting by" without disease. We can expect to have more than just the minimal energy for barely making it through the day. We should be able to play with the children, enjoy our favorite recreation, or have a wonderful romantic night with our spouse even after a long day at work. Modern health care that embraces the concept of Possibility Living strives for the maximum out of life, not the minimum.

Often in my practice, I see people who say that they don't feel sick, but on the other hand they just don't feel right. I hear how they come home from work totally exhausted and eat a dinner they are too tired to enjoy. Then they watch television dozing off in the middle of mindless programming. Finally they fall into bed with a spouse they have fallen out of love with sometime long ago.

Just getting by is for amoebas. The Scriptures say that we should have life, and have it in abundance. Simply not being sick is no longer good enough. Passion and purpose in all aspects of life can be attained when we live a life removed of spiritual, emotional, and physical blockages. Life then becomes this incredible journey of growth and development filled with possibilities for living and void of limitations, as God intended.

PROGRESSIVE WELLNESS EMBODIES POSSIBILITY LIVING

With Possibility Living, we begin a path of fully functioning: physically, emotionally, and spiritually. In Scripture, Jesus kept increasing in wisdom (intellectually), stature (physically), and in relation with God (spiritually) and man (socially; Luke 2:52). Jesus' life models how we can live an ever increasing dynamic, powerful, and purposeful life, utilizing our unlimited spiritual potential while living in a limited physical body.

Progressive developmental wellness is a gift from above. Progressive wellness is an ongoing journey toward the path of fulfilling our God-given potential, as was modeled for us in Luke 2:52. We receive this gift of grace by faith. Wellness is not something necessarily dependent on us; it is a gift from God—we just need to get out of the way. Drs. Joe Flesia and Guy Reikeman talked about this concept of Possibility Living almost thirty years ago when they preached, "Nature needs no help, just no resistance." Progressive, possibility health care takes people from where they are, removes the "resistance," and facilitates abundant living so that they can reach as close to the maximum expression of their God-given potential as possible. In order for us to understand the process of moving away from a health-care model that simply treats symptoms to Possibility Living, we need to go back a few thousand years and look at the early health-care paradigms. Let's take a brief historical journey through health care and the development of the traditional medical model.

Hippocrates. Although Hippocrates is called the father of Western medicine, his philosophy is very dissimilar to what we traditionally see in a doctor's office today. Possibility Living is a renaissance of the vitalistic approach to health and healing that Hippocrates advocated in fifth-century B.C. Greece. Its vital premise is that there is an intelligence far greater than ours who knows far more than we do about how the body functions and maintains health.

The Scriptures tell us, "Greater is he that is in me, than he that is in the world" (1 John 4:4). Hippocrates believed that humans were internally equipped to heal disease through the body's natural forces. He has been quoted as saying, "When in dis-ease, look first to the spine." He felt that there was a life force that resides within, which he called, in Greek, *pneuma*, from which we derive the words "spirit" and "soul." This life force was the critical ingredient to health, and the lack of it the cause of illness. The concept was later referred to as *vis medicatrix naturae*, translated to mean "the healing power of nature."

Galen. The Roman physician Galen (ca. A.D. 129–199) continued the concepts propagated by Hippocrates and promoted the relationship between the mind and the body. He theorized that in 60 percent of the patients he treated, emotional issues interfered with the life force, hence causing illness.

Galen was known to have said, "I bind the wound, God heals it." Today the mantra of many chiropractors is, "I move the bone to release the power, God does the healing." This concept remained popular until the 1600s. Then people with an increased knowledge of the body put more credence in observable facts than in the existence of a life force that could not be verified by concrete evidence. The idea that immaterial thought could somehow have an effect on the physical was considered too mystical at the time. The body was viewed more as a machine, with observable functions in all of its parts. This allowed for the mystery of bodily function to be replaced by a mechanistic view of the body.

Descartes. The French philosopher René Descartes (1596–1650) further developed what we call today the "mechanistic model." This served two very important issues of the time. First, mechanism helped pave the way for the scientific method based on observable facts. Second, Descartes was able to resolve the ongoing conflict between the Roman Catholic church and physicians. The church wanted to keep the human body sacred, considering it to be a reflection of God. Physicians, however, wanted to continue to research into how the human body worked. The primary way to study the body's function was to dissect corpses, which had no life force, and study the parts as pieces. Descartes philosophically separated the mind from the body. He convinced the church that the mind was where the spiritual nature resides, and the body was purely physical. This gave full freedom to physicians to do as they wished with the body.

Newton. Later the English scientist Sir Isaac Newton (1642–1727) cemented this mechanistic view of the body in medical thought. The new Newtonian law of physics was based on a concept of physical laws governing both the universe and the human body. This concept of the mechanistic model continues today in traditional medicine. The body's function could be compared to that of a watch. If we had a broken watch, all we would need to do was take it apart, look for the part that was causing the problem, and then remove or replace it. After fixing what was broken, the watch would then work as before.

Today, as a result of this mechanistic paradigm, if a tonsil, ovary, or gall bladder causes discomfort, the solution is simply to remove the bad piece. However, we believe that the body is greater than the sum of its parts. We believe that the body does function as a whole and that every part of the body has an influence on every other part of the body. God didn't create us with unnecessary, useless organs and tissues.

We understand that only life heals. While I was in graduate school, we were required to perform many cadaver dissections. Not once did I ever see a cadaver heal from the cuts we made. The famous physician, scholar, and theologian Dr. Albert Schweitzer said the body must have life for the ability to heal.[8] As a doctor who deals with illness and healing, I see how miraculous this God-given power of life is to heal and restore bodily functions.

GOD'S POSSIBILITIES FOR HEALTH ARE WITHIN US

Doctors can provide treatment for patients from the outside. For example, we can put a splint on a fractured arm. The arm can even be set if it is displaced. However, the splinting or the setting, in and of itself, does not bring about healing. Although it is a beneficial act to attempt a cure, we must also remove any blockages so that the body can express more life and healing can ultimately occur.

I will remember Ann for a long time. One busy afternoon in my chiropractic office one of my staff asked me if I could come to the phone and handle an urgent call. Ann's mother was on the line explaining how her daughter had been taken to the hospital the night before because she was not breathing normally. The parents had become increasingly alarmed when her skin tone turned an ash blue.

The hospital staff helped her out of the critical situation and Ann was not in a life-threatening condition anymore. But the traditional medical model of treatment was unable to help her heal and return to a full life. Her mother asked, "Is there anything you can do?"

"Does she need any further first aid?" I asked. Ann did not need further critical-care attention, so her doctors gave permission for her to be transported to my office. When I had first observed this toddler some time before, she was a very active little girl. Now I saw a very pale, sick girl who was barely conscious, lying in the arms of her father. Her dad said the doctors had done everything they could. Almost in desperation, her parents asked, "What can you do?"

I went through my analysis, determined there was brain stem pressure from cervical dysfunction, and then proceeded to adjust her spine and relieve the nerve pressure. I then told the family I could not say how much this would help; we had to wait and see. After a short period of time, the electronic monitoring system indicated that Ann had made a slight improvement. So I adjusted her two more times, and her readings improved markedly. I then told the emotionally and physically exhausted parents, "That's all we can do for now. Let's see how she responds."

Since the mother was under tremendous stress, I suggested she receive an adjustment as well. As we were about to leave for another treatment room, Ann turned to her father and asked, "Daddy, can I be let down?" It was the first time she had uttered a word in two days. The color of her skin had been mostly restored, life had returned, and she was on her way to being healed. Nothing was broken inside her body that could or should have been replaced from the outside. All she needed was the restoration of the natural healing energy within her, which in her case flowed over the nervous system, so that her body could return from a state of disorganization to reorganization. This natural healing energy is the power that enables the body to heal itself.

When we recognize that within each one of us is the capacity to heal, we can begin to get a grasp of the gift given by God. The Bible says, "For you created my inmost being; you knit me together in my mother's womb. I praise you because I am fearfully and wonderfully made; your works are wonderful, I know that full well" (Ps. 139:13–14, NIV).

We can understand being knit by God for forty weeks in the womb. What surprises most people is that God stays on the job continually reknitting our bodies with the same amazing miraculous power that initially formed our bodies from two cells. Between birth and death, our bodies are in a constant state of breaking down and being healed. Every tissue in the body is continually being restored and renewed under the supervision of the nervous system. Every cell is in its own particular regeneration process. Some cells take longer than others, but nonetheless they will renew or be discarded by a healthy body.

As I mentioned at the beginning of this chapter, we could live to 120 years with vitality just like Moses'. God created us for optimal function for a vital 100 or more years. Genesis 1:26 tells us that we were created in his image. His image is perfect, expressing life in abundance, not lack or dysfunction. Our bodies, minds, and spirits should then reflect his image. Our trips to the doctor should be to get checked for optimal function and not just the presence of disease. We can learn from those who focus on maintaining wellness how to care for our bodies by avoiding toxins and making right choices about eating and exercise.

The rest of this book is about how to do just that. Our prayer for you, the reader, is that you will understand and accept Possibility Living for yourself—body, mind, and spirit. You were created for God's purposes to live an abundant life. We pray that you will be a good steward of the temple you were given. Let God's creative and healing wisdom of the body serve you by removing all the toxic substances, stress, people, and habits that could prevent you from enjoying the maximum expression of life. Allow God's power, which made your body, to maintain and heal it.

We hope to motivate you toward the preservation of health, so you may enjoy a long and vital life, rich in possibilities. Disease is merely the absence of health. Choose health. Choose life. Choose Possibility Living!

CHAPTER 3

POSSIBILITY LIVING MAKES RIGHT CHOICES

Dr. Robert A. Schuller

Possibility Living is a gift from God. It begins with the gift of life, continues with the gift of possibilities, and is fulfilled with the gift of eternal life. Life itself is a gift, not a right. The fact that we wake up every morning able to breathe is one of the greatest gifts we have. That alone is a reason for us to be thankful to God. Thankfulness then becomes the launching pad for Possibility Thinking.

If we can make the right holistic choices, the result will be a long, healthy, and eternal life. Making the right choices is the foundation upon which we begin a journey to Possibility Living. Life is not just existing—it's much more! Possibility Living will enable you to make right choices so that you will

- live prosperously and productively

- pray effectively

- hear and obey the Spirit's leading

- enjoy health as a lifestyle

- eat the right kind of food

- create a healthy environment

- discover how Christ transforms the negative into the positive

- think positively and associate with positive people

- read God's signs all around you

This kind of life becomes possible when we make the choice to accept God's love. For some, perhaps for you as well, it may be difficult to accept the love of God. There are those who have experienced so many difficulties that they no longer feel any self-worth and therefore do not feel worthy of the gift of God's love.

"Why would God give anything to me?" they retort.

"God loves me?" they shout.

"Do you realize where I have been? What I've done? What I am?" they protest.

Right now while reading these words, you can become a new person—a new creation.

You can receive a new paradigm of living that will give you the spiritual fitness to overcome the negatives in life. Remember that the symbol of Christianity is a cross. The cross is the negative turned into a positive. It is the minus sign turned into a plus sign. You can begin to live when you realize the promises of God. Listen to these promises:

- For God so loved the world, that he gave his only begotten Son, that whosoever believeth in him should not perish, but have everlasting life (John 3:16, NLT).

- For I know the plans I have for you, says the Lord. They are plans for good and not for disaster, to give you a future and a hope. In those days when you pray, I will listen, says the Lord (Jer. 29:11–12).

- For if you confess with your mouth that Jesus is Lord and believe in your heart that God raised him from the dead, you will be saved. For it is by believing in your heart that you are made right with God, and it is by confessing with your mouth that you are saved (Rom. 10:9–10).

- My purpose is to give life in all its fullness. I am the good shepherd. The good shepherd lays down his life for the sheep (John 10:10–11).

- Praise the Lord. He forgives all my sins and heals all my diseases. He ransoms me from death and surrounds me with love and tender mercies. He fills my life with good things. My youth is renewed like the eagle's! (Ps. 103:1–5).

- All things work together for good to those who love God, to those who are called according to his purpose (Rom. 8:28).

Do you want to be a follower of Jesus Christ? This is the first and most important choice you will need to make when moving into Possibility Living. If you do, pray this prayer:

Dear Jesus,

You promise that you have a plan for my life today.

You promise that you will forgive my sins.

You promise that you will give me eternal life.

You promise that you will be with me forever.

You promise that you will help me through the toughest of times.

You promise that you will turn all things into good.

You promise that you will do all this for me

If I will simply accept your love and forgiveness from above and allow it to come down and enter my soul.

If I give myself to you, and let your love live in me and flow out of me in loving others.

If I choose to accept you as Lord and Savior and to live in your possibilities.

Lord, your offer sounds like a good deal. I accept!! Thank you for giving everything to me. For my life, today and tomorrow. For a future of hope, possibilities, life, and health. Let your power flow from above down into me, live inside of me through Your Spirit and flow out of me in Possibility Living. Give me the faith to believe in you and to continue to live with your promises before me forever and ever. Amen.

The minute you offer yourself to God in prayer, you will start receiving his abundant possibilities for your life.

A biblical principle is that by giving we receive. This is one of the great paradoxes of life. When we give our life to God, God gives it right back to us. How amazing and awesome. God asks you and me, "What would you do if you knew you could not fail?" By embracing God's possibilities and being guided by his Spirit we can make the right choices and begin to mature into the type of person that God wants us to be and we want to become.

CHOOSE A PROSPEROUS AND PRODUCTIVE LIFE

As you begin the joy of Possibility Living, you will understand the essential need that all of us have to develop a relationship with God. As our relationship with God matures, so does our health and wholeness. Self-reliance pursues a path full of pitfalls and dangers. There are no promises. Nothing is secure. The prophet Isaiah said it this way: "All flesh is grass and all its loveliness is like the flower of the field. The grass withers and the flower fades when the breath of the Lord blows upon it. Surely the people are grass. The grass withers and the flower fades but the word of God stands forever" (Isa. 40:6–8). Only God's promises are sure and lasting. Thus the old expression: "All things in life will pass, only what's done for Christ will last." How do we measure our effectiveness in life?

Many years ago my father wrote a book entitled *The Peak to Peek Principle*. In his book, Robert H. Schuller shared with us how one victory leads to another. The best analogy for understanding the peak-to-peek principle is to climb a mountain.

I will never forget the first time I ascended a mountain near Big Bear Lake, California. When my father received a small inheritance following the death of his mother, he took this money and bought an "unbuildable" lot near Big Bear Lake in the San Bernardino Mountains of California. As with many things in my father's life, he never takes no for an answer. He promptly began to build a beautiful cabin on this "unbuildable" location, which he has since given to the ministry.

One day as I was sitting in that cabin looking at the mountain peak, I decided I would climb it. I thought I could ascend it in a short course of time. So I began my hike. It seemed like it would be a very easy hike as I reached the first peak. Looking up, peeking, from that peak, I soon realized there was a valley to cross and another peak to climb on my way to the top. I climbed down that valley and ascended the next peak. I was about to celebrate my victory, when I "peeked" a new peak with a valley in front of me. So I continued on my way until I ran out of time. I learned that in order to climb that mountain, I had to go peak by peek.

The peak-to-peek principle shows us that it is possible to ascend to a level of success, and from that level to see an even greater success before us. And from that next success we are able to see a still greater success before us, one that prior to our first accomplishment was not even imaginable. And so it proceeds, as we live our life going from peak to peek, to peak to peek...

In order to live peak to peek, we need a perspective on where we are going that is higher and wiser than our own. At times, the peaks ahead of us may be clouded by emotions, attitudes, circumstances, or obstacles. But there is One who sees through every cloud even in the misty future. God knows the plans he has for us and reveals them to us through possibility prayer.

CHOOSE TO PRAY EFFECTIVELY

Possibility prayer is a two-way supernatural conversation. If we follow the example that Christ gave us in his prayer, the Lord's Prayer, we learn that the first thing we need to give God is praise. Praise is an expression of faith, worship, and peace. It is the act of thankfulness for God's forgiveness and unconditional love.

Then with a thankful heart we can offer up petitions. So our petitions are actually God-inspired desires. We seek God's will for our life and discover that God's will and our will are usually the same thing. In this way God gives us the desires of our heart. These desires reflect what is best for us in living the possibility-filled life.

In praying we are to model Jesus. Jesus taught in John 12:49, "For I did not speak on My own initiative, but the Father Himself who sent Me has given Me commandment, what to say, and what to speak" (NAS). The Holy Spirit promised us he would do the same. As in all other aspects of our life, we must rely on the Holy Spirit from above to flow down from the Father and lead us in prayer. Even when we don't know what to pray, God's Spirit prays effectively through us, guiding us in God's possibility plan for us.

CHOOSE TO HEAR AND OBEY THE SPIRIT'S LEADING

One of the most beautiful promises we have received from God is the promise of a "Comforter." The Holy Spirit of God was sent into the world to guide, teach, comfort, and counsel us. Jesus tells us, "And I will ask the Father, and he will give you another Counselor to be with you forever—the Spirit of truth. The world cannot accept him, because it neither sees him nor knows him. But you know him, for he lives with you and will be in you" (John 14:16–17, NIV).

Notice that the Spirit lives in us. He comes from above, down to us, so that he may live in us and flow out of us with God's power and love. But how does God live in and through us without making us into puppets and hampering our free will? God is sovereign, and yet God allows us freely to make choices in life.

One of the fundamentals of theology is God's sovereignty. God is only God if he is sovereign. If he isn't sovereign, then he is something other than God. The word "God" means Almighty Ruler, King of All Things, Omnipotent One. These important questions come to mind:

> So if God is the master controller of all that is, then what is our role?
>
> Are we puppets on a string?
>
> Are we nothing more than "worms," to quote John Calvin, the sixteenth-century Reformer?
>
> Do we have the ability or free will to do anything?
>
> Is it safe to have a relationship with someone who is so controlling?
>
> Do I, or can I, take responsibility, blame, or credit for anything I say or do since God is in control?

These are important questions, probably the most important questions you can ever ask yourself, more important even than "Who am I going to marry?" or "What am I going to do with the rest of my life?"

The reality of the sovereignty of God really hit me when I took a class in seminary on the writings of Calvin. As a theologian, John Calvin wrote volumes of essays, commentaries on the Bible, and his most famous work, *The Institutes of the Christian Religion*. A "Calvinist" is one who, among other things, places a very strong emphasis on the sovereignty of God. God is sovereign to the point that God elects whom he will save by inviting them into his family and whom he will condemn to hell (in theological circles that is called double predestination). There is no free will involved. If you are not chosen, well, you loose. It was that black-and-white for John Calvin.

On the other hand, what about our ability to control our lives and make decisions?

What motivation to succeed and better ourselves do we have?

Are we allowed to tie our shoes without the directions of God?

Does God make us sin?

Is God responsible for my evil ways?

Why does God allow bad things to happen to good people?

Why does God make me sick?

Why did God give me such weak genes?

St. Augustine said, "Pray like it all depends on God and work like it all depends on you!" This has been for me a prescription for living that combines the sovereignty of God with human free will. It doesn't answer all our questions, but it does tell us how we are to live in spite of our questions. This book can answer many of them and will do so as we proceed. Possibility Living puts the responsibility on each of us to "work out our salvation" (Phil. 2:12). To do so, we need to make right choices guided by God's Spirit in every aspect of life—body, mind, and spirit.

CHOOSE HEALTH AS A LIFESTYLE

Health is a journey, not a destination. Health as a lifestyle begins the day we are born and continues until that day we stand face-to-face with Jesus Christ.

I have four children. My oldest was born in 1976 and my youngest in 1986. I'll never forget the birth of my children. I was in the delivery room for each of them. It was a spiritually thrilling experience to see the hand of God creating life. They were all perfectly healthy when they were born and they began to grow almost instantly. Birth is miraculous.

After birth, the first thing the nurses did was to take the children away and put them through a battery of blood tests. They put medication in their eyes, cleaned them up, and then handed them back to us. As our children grew, we did our best to be good parents. As prescribed by the pediatrician, we had the vaccinations on schedule. When they had a runny nose, we brought them in, received the prescriptions of antibiotics, and administered them to our children meticulously.

Unfortunately, my boys didn't do very well as young children. My older son, Bobby, had chronic ear infections. He ultimately had major surgery to remove his tonsils and adenoids and to place tubes in his ears. It did little good, as the ear infections continued. My younger son, Anthony, was on the same path Bobby was on. He had chronic ear infections and in addition he had asthma. We went to the emergency room numerous times with a "blue" child. It was very dangerous and scary. By the grace of God he survived.

It was at that time that my wife started going to Dr. Michael Shalhoub, a chiropractor, for back pain. She had scoliosis in her spine. He told her he needed to see the entire family. When Donna mentioned that I needed to go and see him, I thought she had really misunderstood my situation. I didn't have any back pain—I was in "perfect heath."

The truth was that I had chronic sinus infections. I was taking antibiotics every month. My nose and throat were filled with mucous. It made me hoarse and I spoke in a nasal tone. For a pastor and preacher, that is not good. Every Christmas Eve and Easter I knew that I would be coughing and sneezing and wondering how I would make it through the next four or five services.

Wives can be very persuasive, or at least mine is, and she insisted that I go to the chiropractor. Of course I went to make her feel better. He took some X rays and showed me that my spine needed some work. He also informed me that he could help me with my sinus infections.

The next week I saw my friendly pharmacist, Bernie, and told him that I was going to a chiropractor. He asked, "Do you have back problems?"

"No," I said, "but he thinks he can help me with my sinus infections."

"Help you with your sinus? What does sinus have to do with your back?"

With that he became angry and said, "I wish those &#%! chiropractors would just treat the back and quit trying to cure everything!"

That was one of the last times I saw him. Not because he became angry, but because we now rely on God's plan for health through Possibility Living rather than always using medications. Why was my pharmacist angry? He lost a customer. We used to spend thousands of dollars annually on prescriptions and medications. Among the six of us, we saw him once or twice a week. Now we see our chiropractor instead.

Going to see Dr. Michael Shalhoub began my transition from traditional medicine to modern wellness. It was the fork in the road that led to health. As Robert Frost writes in his poem "The Road Not Taken":

I shall be telling this with a sigh
Somewhere ages and ages hence:
Two roads diverged in a wood, and I—
I took the one less traveled by,
And that has made all the difference.

This book may become your fork in the road that leads to health and wellness.

Through it, you can achieve a physical state that launches you into vitality for the rest of your life. Health is a journey that begins by getting on the right road and continues by making the conscious decisions that enhance wellness. One practical step you can take immediately is deciding to eat right and embrace a fit lifestyle.

CHOOSE THE RIGHT FOODS

One of the big challenges we have in life is to eat healthy food. We learn to enjoy food because it tastes good. We judge it not by its nutritional benefits, but by the texture, sight, smell, and taste. If it meets these requirements, then it must be good. It is very difficult to go to a restaurant and find a menu that gives the nutritional information necessary to determine whether certain foods are "good food" or "food good for us."

Food that is good for us nourishes the body. That is its primary goal. It should also give pleasure though taste and comfort, but that is not its chief function. We do not live to eat, but rather we eat to live. However, it is the former that concerns most consumers. Therefore, most suppliers, restaurants, and grocers are typically more concerned about the presentation and portions of the servings than the food value. That is because their clientele have prescribed the need. When we make a choice of what to eat, we need to make the decisions that choose life and health.

Eat God's food. Possibility Living uses God's food instead of "man's" food. It's Daniel's diet versus the king's diet:

> Daniel said to the steward, "Please test your servants for ten days, and let them give us vegetables to eat and water to drink. Then let our appearance be examined before you, and the appearance of the young men who eat the portion of the king's delicacies; and as you see fit so deal with your servants." So he consented with them in this matter and tested them ten days. And at the end of ten days their features appeared better and fatter in flesh than all the young men who ate the portion of the king's delicacies. As for these young men, God gave them knowledge and skill in all literature and wisdom.
>
> Daniel 1:11–17

The mainstays of the current king's diet are Burger King, Dairy Queen, and Imperial Margarine. God's diet consists of unprocessed, natural foods like fruits, vegetables, and water. All diet choices have consequences. Eating the king's diet for a long period of time produces sickness, poisoning, malnutrition, and premature death. Eating God's food produces life and fills us with the potential for Possibility Living.

Eat God's food; don't eat the king's food. The purpose of the king's food is profit. It will benefit him financially while you go unfed. Your tummy will feel full, but your body will scream for nourishment. The closer you can get to eating what God produces, the better it is for you.

So fresh, organic, vine-ripened whole foods are the best. As soon as we start manipulating the food, like using artificial fertilizers, the nutritional value of the food diminishes. You'll pay a little bit more for some things. For example, you'll pay more for the pure maple syrup rather than the bottle of maple-flavored corn-sugar, but you'll pay a lot less for a bag of apples than a bag of potato chips. You'll probably be dollars ahead in your food budget and years ahead in your life budget.

Foods that have life give life.

On my radio program, I interviewed nutritionist Elizabeth Baker, who has a written numerous "uncook" cookbooks. She teaches people how to prepare raw fruits, nuts, and vegetables. She wants these "live" foods to look appetizing and taste good, and she has some very good ideas in her books on how to do that.

From her I learned that raw foods have enzymes, complex proteins that act as catalysts for certain biochemical reactions. Enzymes are "alive." They are what make seeds germinate. They are a scientific reality—many biochemical reactions cannot occur without them.

Enzymes are the enemy of mass food distributors. They cause the food on the shelves to continue the organic process that begins after food has been harvested—it begins to rot. Without them the food on the shelves can last much longer, creating a much greater profit margin because there is no waste to throw away.

Have you noticed that if you take food that is about to go bad and cook it, it will last a few more days? That is because you killed the enzymes when you cooked it.

Our bodies need enzymes to function properly. We need them to digest our food. God put them in our food so that we can turn the substance we put into our mouths into nourishment. Live food is food rich with enzymes. We need to eat it raw because enzymes die when the temperature reaches 120 degrees.

The more you cook your food the more enzyme-deficient your food becomes. Uncooked vegetables and fruits are essential to good health. We need to eat several portions of enzyme-rich foods every day. We suggest that you eat something raw or live with every meal and snack. It is a rule in our families.

CHOOSE TO CREATE A HEALTHY ENVIRONMENT

The choices we make in life will create the environment we live in. "You reap what you sow." This truth originates in one of Jesus' parables. In his parable of the sower, he shares with us the results of sowing good seed:

> A farmer went out to sow his seed. As he was scattering the seed, some fell along the path, and the birds came and ate it up. Some fell on rocky places, where it did not have much soil. It sprang up quickly, because the soil was shallow. But when the sun came up, the plants were scorched, and they withered because they had no root. Other seed fell among thorns, which grew up and choked the plants. Still other seed fell on good soil, where it produced a crop—a hundred, sixty or thirty times what was sown.
>
> Matthew 13:3–8, NIV

This parable illustrates how important it is to plant seeds of success—ones that will produce a healthy and prosperous life. What keeps us from attaining this desired harvest?

Within each of us lies a champion. The only difference between the champions and the defeated is the way that each responds to failure. Those who have attained the prize are those who have learned to use for good what they encounter in the environment.

Our environment is not what surrounds us as much as it is our perception of our surroundings. Humans as a species are unique in their ability to reason. This God-given gift has put us above all other living creatures. "Rule over every living creature," the Bible says (Gen. 1:28). This gift has also created within us a unique challenge—the capacity for foresight or imagination. A pessimist will look to the future with fear and skepticism, while an optimist, given the same facts, will see a bright and hopeful tomorrow.

Mark Twain said, "Most of us spend much of our time worrying about things that never happen." This added stress causes premature aging. The most constructive way to combat anxiety is by choosing to create a healthy mental environment. This happens when we look to

God and remember the wonderful words of Jesus in the Sermon on the Mount:

> Therefore I tell you, do not worry about your life, what you will eat or drink; or about your body, what you will wear. Is not life more important than food and the body more important than clothes? Look at the birds of the air; they do not sow or reap or store away in barns, and yet your heavenly Father feeds them. Are you not much more valuable that they? Who of you by worrying can add a single hour to his life?
>
> Matthew 6:25–27

Creating a healthy environment begins with a healthy, positive, optimistic outlook on life.

CHOOSE CHRIST, WHO TRANSFORMS THE NEGATIVE INTO THE POSITIVE

The death of Jesus on the cross transformed the most negative thing in life into a positive. He took death and turned it into life. He took sin and turned it into good. He took nothing and turned it into something. That is the miracle of the cross.

A Galilean dying on a cross didn't seem all that significant at the time. Thousands of people were crucified. Many lingered for days on the cross before dying, but Jesus died quickly. The death was not what made the historical event so traumatic. It was the spiritual reality behind the scene that makes the cross so meaningful and beautiful.

On the cross, Jesus suffered the greatest pain known to human beings—he was rejected by his father. "My God, my God, why have you forsaken me?" (Mark 15:34). Never before in the history of humankind had God rejected anyone. Throughout the Bible God seemed to have abandoned his people, but always came back to them. At just the moment when it looked like God was absent and all was lost, God saved and delivered the people from destruction.

When it looked like

- all humanity would be drowned in the flood, God saved Noah's family, a faithful remnant

- all of Israel would be mired in perpetual slavery, God brought Israel out of bondage in Egypt, through the Red Sea, and into freedom

- all the Israelites would die in the wilderness, wandering aimlessly there for forty years, God used Joshua to lead them into the promised land

- all the tribes of Israel would be destroyed by the Philistines, God raised up mighty judges like Samson, Gideon, and Deborah to defeat their enemies

- all of the Hebrews would be forever exiled by Babylon, God brought them back to rebuild the Temple under Nehemiah and Ezra

- God's only son, Jesus, would die on the cross and with him all hope and salvation be lost, God raised him from the dead, filling time and eternity with limitless and living possibilities

Now we know that God never leaves or forsakes us (Heb. 13:5). Jesus as the extension of God himself is accepting the sins of all humankind from the beginning of time to the end. That is one of the reasons he is called the Alpha and the Omega. It is this sin that God rejects, and as the Apostles' Creed declares, Jesus "descended into hell." Heaven is "being with God," and hell is "separation from God."

God separated himself from Jesus on the cross. Jesus descended into hell. There he paid the price for sin, conquered death and hell, and rose again to sit enthroned on the right hand of God. Jesus took the negative of sin and turned it into the most positive thing the world has ever seen. That is why the written and spoken accounts of Jesus are called the Gospels, or Good News.

God's good news for you proclaims and promises that God wants to help you create a healthy environment that will turn your negatives into positives. He will do that one thought at a time and one day at a time as we grow with him. It takes time. Remember, the weeds are the first things to sprout in your garden. The flowers and the trees take a little longer.

The challenge you have now is to respond positively to the voice of God. He calls every one. He calls us in different ways. Some have claimed to have heard the audible voice of God. I have been told, "It is as if someone were in the room with me." I have not had this experience. If God wanted to, he would talk to you or me in that manner. He hasn't promised that he would, so I won't hold my breath, and I suggest you don't either.

Instead, listen to God speaking to you in these ways:

1. Listen to positive thoughts.

2. Listen to positive people.

3. Read the Bible.

4. Read the signs of the times pointing to where God is at work around you.

It is difficult to listen to positive thoughts because first we have to filter out all the negative ones that race through our heads and lead to discouragement and despair.

CHOOSE POSITIVE THOUGHTS AND PEOPLE

Positive thoughts are one of the primary ways God talks to us. He gives us ideas and hopes, dreams and aspirations. If these thoughts are healthy, positive, and constructive, they are God thoughts or God ideas. The thoughts that are not from God are greedy, self-serving, and contrary to God's laws. God created this world and knows what it takes to make it work for you. Follow his commands from the Bible and you will not go wrong. In my book *In Search of Morality*, I explain how this works. We need to translate these God ideas into goals to which we commit ourselves. As we follow these, we allow the Holy Spirit to guide us as he has promised.

The challenge of following through on God's positive ideas for us can be very scary. It can be terrifying to think of what might be expected of us. Then fear grips us and we do nothing. I believe the greatest sin of all is to do nothing.

I am reminded of the time I took my son and some of the boys from our school out on a snorkeling trip. There were so many excuses; you never heard so many excuses in all your life why they couldn't do it. We got all of them out there, and in our particular group there were three boys who had a problem. One wouldn't go at all. The other two couldn't figure out this snorkel-and-mask thing to save their lives. So I stayed behind with them, figuring that I could help them because I had snorkeled before. I thought, "I'll hang with these kids and see if I can help them and get them out so they can see some ocean life and fish, so they are not just like a cork out there bobbing along having a miserable day. They won't learn anything that way."

The first thing I said was, "Boys, you have to put your face in the water. But first put the mask over your nose, put the snorkel in your mouth and breathe through your mouth, not your nose." So, we went through all the particulars about snorkeling and I told them to get their faces in the water where they could see something.

When they actually put their faces in the water and were looking at the sand, they said, "This is cool. I can see the sand."

I said, "I know, isn't this neat?"

With them holding on to the boogie board, I started paddling out a little bit farther off shore, but as soon as they realized we started going farther out, one boy jumped off and said, "Hey, where are you going?"

I replied, "We're going out a little bit deeper."

He said, "No, no, I'm not going deeper."

I said, "I'll tell you what, I'll take you out, your friend can stay here, and then I'll come back for him." So one stayed, looking at the sand and paddling around. The other one, very reluctantly and very scared, said, "I don't want to go in the deep water."

"Okay, we won't go in the deep water; we'll stay very close to shore." Well, we followed the shoreline by the rocks. As we went along, soon we saw a fish. I said to him, "Every time you see a fish, you point to him. Don't take your head out of the water, because the snorkel will go into the water and you'll start breathing the water. Keep your face in the water and just point, and I'll see your hands."

As we drifted along, he kept pointing at fish. And we're having a wonderful time. He was lying on top of a boogie board, I was holding on to it, and I was right next to him. He was secure, had a wetsuit on, and it was impossible for him to go under the water even if he tried. All of a sudden he realized he couldn't touch the bottom. Out comes his head and he screams, "It's deep, it's deep, and I've got to get out of here . . . It's deep, it's deep!"

"Okay, okay." So, we turned around and we went back to shore.

The second boy was back on the shore, playing in the sand and snorkeling around; he had it all figured out. So I said, "Okay, Sean, let's go!"

He said, "No, I'm not going!"

A teacher on the shore said, "Sean, you go with Dr. Schuller. He's a certified diver so you're in good hands. You go with him and he'll take care of you. You know how to snorkel, you've been practicing here."

Sean said, "No, I'm not going."

The teacher cajoled, "I'll give you five merits if you'll go with him."

"No, I'm not going," he asserted.

"I'll take away five demerits." Now, you've got to realize that it is almost impossible to get rid of demerits. "I'll take away five demerits and give you five merits, if you'll just go with Dr. Schuller."

He would not leave. He would not leave the shore regardless of what we offered him, regardless of the safety nets; no matter what we did, he would not go. That was it. It was absolutely amazing.

No matter how able you are and how much God wants to help you, you must choose to think positively or fear will paralyze you. In order to think positive thoughts, you need to associate with positive people.

How do you know the difference between positive and negative people? We often think that the positive people are those who agree with us. If they see things the way we do, then they are positive, and if they disagree with us, then they must be negative.

Positive people are not "yes" people. They can be argumentative and analytical. Yet when they conclude that the decision is right, good, and from God, they have the faith to find the means to succeed. Positive people are people who have faith in God's ability to help them succeed.

CHOOSE TO READ SCRIPTURE

In order for us to really understand the voice of God, we must be in conjunction with God's promises. In order for us to understand his promises and guidance for our lives, we need to read the Bible. The Bible is God's way of communicating with us and revealing himself to us. He chose to communicate verbally with us through the Bible. If you read it, you will experience tremendous guidance, help, and support.

There are several ways to read the Bible. You should choose the one that works best for you.

1. *Start at the beginning:* Many people attempt to read the Bible as if they were going to read a novel. They start at the beginning and usually get stuck around Numbers or Deuteronomy. If you want to read the Bible in this manner, I suggest that you get a chronological Bible. This will make the process somewhat easier, because it puts the text in an order easier for us to understand. The Bible we give to our new members at our church not only puts the text in chronological order, it also divides it into daily reading sections; if you read fifteen minutes a day you will read the entire book in one year.

   If you choose this method, I suggest two things. First, you may wish to start in the New Testament. It is much easier to read and for many it is more encouraging. Second, remember that many people have been reading this book for their entire lives and still don't comprehend everything. So if you want to read the Bible straight through in a year, you will need to leave many questions behind for later.

The chronological Bible is also in a translation that is easy to read. Many people have only read the King James Version of the Bible and do not even realize there are any other options. If you like Shakespearean English, you will like the KJV. Otherwise, get a Bible that is easier to read. Remember that the Bible has been translated from Hebrew and Greek and there are scores of English translations.

2. *Join a bible study:* This is a very good way to read the Bible. You will be systematically lead through different passages and given detailed explanation on how it applies to your life. Most churches have studies available throughout the week.

3. *Read Bible commentaries:* Throughout history scholars have written explanations of every text in the Bible. Many of these are very insightful. The most popular one for laypersons was written by Charles Barkley and is called *Barkley Commentaries.* It is a series of books that takes you through the New Testament. You will find this very helpful regardless of your biblical knowledge.

4. *Read daily devotionals:* Most devotionals start with a Bible verse and then expand on that verse to give you a thought for the day. It is an excellent way of learning the basic fundamentals of Christianity.

READ THE SIGNS

Reading the signs of God is a powerful way to understand and communicate with God. His signs can be intriguing, mysterious, challenging, and frustrating. The signs God gives us need to be interpreted in a positive light, so that we can understand the next step. We need to see that all things "work together for good."

For Thanksgiving 1999, my family went to a small place in Mexico. We had been there before and sized up what we could do for our turkey dinner. Donna, my wife, concluded that the largest turkey we could fit in the oven was an eight-pound turkey. So the week before we left, she bought the little bird and stuck it in the deep freeze. Later that week her mother asked if she could stick her twenty-three-pound thanksgiving bird in our freezer because she didn't have enough room in hers.

I was raised in a large family. I have only seen big turkeys for thanksgiving. So when it was time to leave and Donna asked me to pack the turkey in the cooler, I did. We went to Mexico with everything we needed to cook our Thanksgiving dinner.

On Thanksgiving morning Donna opened the cooler and screamed, "Do you realize what you have done? You took my mother's turkey. She is having tons of people over and all she will have is that glorified chicken. If that isn't bad enough, what are we going to do with that huge thing? It won't fit in the oven."

Well, necessity is the mother of invention. So we did something new for us. I butchered the turkey. I mean, I cut it up into several pieces. We took the breast and put it in our baking dish, and it fit perfectly in the oven. When it came out it was beautiful, moist, and delicious. Then we took the legs, wings, and other pieces and gave them away just like at that first Thanksgiving. We shared our food with some people who were very happy to get this special treat. Meanwhile, Donna's mother had decided to cook chicken for her guests since she didn't have as many people as she thought when she bought the twenty-three pounder. Everything ended well for all concerned.

God cares for everyone. I believe that he had planned the whole thing. He wanted to give some families in Mexico some turkey and he used us to do it.

We can make right choices. Right choices include the following:

- trusting Jesus as Lord and Savior

- praying for the Holy Spirit's direction

- obeying the Holy Spirit's guidance

- choosing to eat God's food

- creating a healthy environment

- cultivating positive thoughts and associating with positive people

- reading the Bible and God's signs

Living A.D.I.O.—*Above, Down, Inside, Out*—will help you make these right choices. In the coming pages, Doug will share with you how living A.D.I.O. will further empower you to make right choices guided by God's Spirit. The power and wisdom to make right choices come from God *above*. His wisdom comes *down* to dwell *inside* us so that it can flow *out* of us, affecting not only our choices in life, but also our relationships with others.

We have the choice to determine how we will react to all circumstances. God has empowered us to react positively or negatively. The choice is yours. Begin living positively now. Possibility Living is filled with positive, right choices that you can make immediately!

CHAPTER 4

CHOOSE TO LIVE A.D.I.O. : ABOVE, DOWN, INSIDE, OUT

Dr. Douglas Di Siena

> We rejoice in the power to be a channel for the expression of divine purpose.
>
> B. J. Palmer, D.C.

Above, Down, Inside, Out (A.D.I.O.)[1] provides a foundation for living your life filled with God's infinite possibilities! In this chapter, we will explore A.D.I.O. in three separate sections—as it applies to body, mind, and spirit.

There is no separation or fragmentation of our being while we are here on earth. There is a spiritual component to something as trivial as a common cold. And when there is a psychological problem confronting us, a physical manifestation or symptom will appear somewhere in our body. Body, mind, and spirit are so interconnected that what happens in one part of us affects the whole person.

In Possibility Living your body will experience health by living from the *inside out*. Your soul will encounter the possibilities of God's love, which comes from *above down*, and then share that love with others from the *inside out*. And your spirit will be empowered to tune into God's possibilities for your life as his power flows from *above* and then *down* through your spirit so that your relationships with him and others can be lived from the *inside out*.

LEARNING TO LIVE A.D.I.O.

What is A.D.I.O.? Here's my testimony of how A.D.I.O. helped me build a foundation for Possibility Living.

Above, Down, Inside, Out changed my life. As a sixteen-year-old boy growing up in a very safe, upper-middle-class suburban neighborhood, I thought all was well with the world. Friends were plentiful as a result of playing on the football team. Both my siblings were now out of the house getting on with their lives. I had one room for study and music (mostly music) and a bedroom, which with the departure of my siblings was now upgraded with a king-sized bed. What could be better? How about a new car as a belated birthday present? I seemed to get from my parents whatever I wanted.

My very generous parents drove me down to a dealership where I pointed to the MG convertible I had dreamed about for months. My mother found out the price, wrote the check, and I drove home a brand-new sports car. Life couldn't get any better.

The summer before my junior year in high school, my chest began to feel tight occasionally. With increasing frequency and intensity, my symptoms grew worse. Any type of exercise caused me to wheeze and experience a shortness of breath. I grew more and more uncomfortable, so my mother took me to the family doctor. He diagnosed my condition as asthma. Immediately I felt uneasy. I thought about my ailing grandmother who lived with a chronic obstructive lung disease. My childhood memories of her were filled with emergency trips to the hospital so my mom could be by her side, fearing that the latest respiratory infection might be more than grandma's body could battle.

When my grandmother was not in the emergency room, she was constantly organizing her multitude of prescriptions or laboriously struggling to breath on her inhaling machine. I certainly did not want to spend the rest of my life living as she did. This kind of chronically ill lifestyle is on the opposite end of the spectrum from Possibility Living.

As the weeks went by, my medical doctor saw me on a more regular basis. He gave me a series of antibiotics followed by corticosteroids, which began to weaken my system. Eventually, I became increasingly dependent on using my inhaler. The side effects of my medications began to take their toll on me emotionally as well as physically. Most of my asthmatic attacks occurred at night, which meant I had to increase my dosages at night. The effect could be compared to drinking the strongest espresso coffee, one cup after another. Not a great method for ensuring a good night's sleep.

During many dark nights, I didn't think I would ever be able to take another breath. My father would stay up with me through the night, occasionally hitting my back as I leaned over the bed in an effort to loosen the mucous congestion clogging my lungs, after which I would get up to puff on my inhaler again in the desperate hope that I would not suffocate. I needed my father to be there almost every night for over a year and a half.

This amphetamine-like effect of the medication caused me to lose weight drastically. My weight plummeted to 143 pounds, a quick loss of almost 40 pounds in just a few months. In addition to the weight loss, the right side of my chest became deformed as a result of the chronic lung obstruction. In the midst of all of this, even with increasing doses of medication, my asthma continued to worsen. I couldn't play sports or even think about playing football. My grades plummeted as quickly as my weight. I had been a favorite of all my teachers, but now they noticed my weight loss, my blurred eyes, and, to make a bad impression worse, my dozing off in school.

The collective opinion of my teachers was that I was another kid lost to the drug scene, which was so prevalent in the 1970s. Those who had seemed to be close friends began to disappear. As a final coup de grace, my brand new MG, only a few months old, blew up! It may seem almost trivial now, but at the time, that car was one of the last bright spots in my life.

How did I recover physically?

The power of God came from *above down* and healed me on the *inside*. My physical healing occurred when I was seventeen, after I had been struggling with my ailment for about a year and a half. At this low point in my life, God directed me to join a gym in an attempt to recover my health. The owner of this gym happened to be a chiropractor. As he signed me up, he asked me if I had ever seen a chiropractor before. I never had, I never "felt the need," but an urgent desire swept over me to explore the possibility.

He took a radiograph of my neck and after analyzing it said, "You lost the normal curve in your neck, putting tension on your brain stem. This could create nerve stress, keeping your brain from effectively communicating with your body." He went on to say that by restoring my curve, the nerve stress would be relieved and I could recreate health where there was now sickness. He then simply asked me if I wanted to get well. For the first time in a long time I was hopeful about my future. I said yes to this man's care. Six weeks later I slept through the night for the first time in almost two years, and within three months I gained most of my weight back and was off all medications. Not only could I take a breath with out a struggle, but I felt as though my entire life had been restored.

Through my sickness, I received not only the gift of healing. One day as I was lying face down on that vinyl adjusting table awaiting the chiropractor, I received a purpose and a vision. The purpose God laid on my heart was the intense desire to return the gift of health God so graciously gave to me to as many people as God would bring my way. The vision of how I was to do this was to lay hands on sick and suffering people primarily through the art of chiropractic in an effort to help them get well.

The only physical effect of my illness that remains with me today is the deformity in my chest, called Harrison's groove, which resulted from the tremendous negative pressure constantly in my chest cavity due to my inability to inhale. Today I see this not as a deformity, but as a mark of God's tremendous grace, love, and healing power. It also serves as a reminder for me. If I ever get tired of telling the A.D.I.O. message or laying on my hands for the purpose of healing illness or maintaining wellness, I just need to look in the mirror, remember my plight, and ponder the many others out there who are needlessly suffering and have lost all hope for their healing.

YOUR BODY: EXPERIENCE HEALTH BY LIVING A.D.I.O.

Physical healing always flows from the inside out. Although it may seem obvious that healing comes from the inside, the traditional medical model still treats from the outside in. One example of the traditional paradigm is the germ theory of disease propagated by Louis Pasteur.

In many ways the discovery of the germ was perhaps responsible for the dramatic increase in life expectancy and drastic decrease in morbidity. Now you might be thinking that I contradict myself. Let me explain. Sanitation, as a result discovering germs, helped us detoxify our environment. This dramatically decreased the stress on our immune systems. It wasn't until just a few centuries ago that people stopped dumping their waste where they lived, ate, and drank.

If we accept the idea that germs cause disease, it would make sense to cleanse not only our body, but the planet as well. This kind of thinking has led to the massive overuse of pharmaceuticals. The idea of germs causing disease removes any responsibility from us for taking care of ourselves physically.

The truth is, the germ theory is of no use in an attempt to heal the body. The germ theory keeps us looking on the outside for an invader that makes our bodies ill. I find it interesting that even Pasteur believed germs could be held in check within natural law. He believed that when the host, or the body, is strong, germs would not make the body ill. In a weak body, however, germs are able to invade and flourish.

As we have mentioned previously, a person residing in a state of health and wholeness is not as susceptible to disease. Or put another way, people are not sick because they have a disease; they have a disease because they are already sick. Our bodies will not manifest disease unless we have already abandoned optimal life expression and entered the realm of sickness.

Today, we see modern science revealing some very contradictory evidence with respect to the germ theory of disease. The 1969 Pulitzer Prize winner Dr. René J. Dubos, who is very widely respected as a prominent bacteriologist, has illustrated just how weak the argument for the germ theory of disease is. Bacteriologists have shown us that humans are not the only ones with the ability to adapt to the environment; all living organisms have the capacity to sustain life and to propagate their own because of the ability to adapt physiologically.

The alarming increase in the number of antibiotic-resistant bacteria leads us to question where we will end up if we continue to follow the current path. Some of these harmless bacteria that were just yesteryear's nuisances now have the virulence to kill. How many cover stories in major news magazines do we need to see before we choose to build up our own internal defenses? The May 10, 1999, issue of *U.S. News and World Report*, in an article called "The Battle of the Bugs," revealed that in up to 40 percent of the pneumococcal infections presented to doctors the bacteria have adapted to their environment in such a drastic way that they have become immune to our strongest antibiotic therapies.

Scientists tell us that some of these antibiotic-resistant bacteria not only survive the antibiotics, but thrive on them. They actually flourish by consuming antibiotics. Germs are very much like scavengers. They have a vital role in the cleanup of toxic tissue. They need dead or diseased organic tissue for their survival. Yet it is not until there is an overwhelmingly toxic environment that the bacteria cause a problem.

Germs are merely opportunistic conveyors of disease, not the cause. Worse yet, by killing the weakest bacteria, we are left with the strongest, most deadly bacteria to fight. In essence, we are killing off the bugs that won't do us harm, only to then weaken our immune system, leaving us more susceptible to the infection of the more vicious germs. This results in an epidemic of virulent, hard-to-kill, deadly germs. We have spent time, money, and lives fighting the wrong battle, one we can never win. Although antibiotics have certainly benefited humanity as a first aid or for crisis care, we abused the therapy to the point of our potential demise.

If my backyard were infested with rodents, I would be far better off removing the garbage (the cause) than attempting to kill the entire rodent population. Bacteriologists, as well as other prominent scientists, now point toward ways to clean up and detoxify the body instead of using drugs to eliminate all the germs.

God designed nature for survival. God has arranged everything in a very tight, complex balance. Germs will adapt to whatever type of antibiotic we can throw at them. They will adapt; their physiology will mutate for purposes of survival. That is what germs do. God designed it that way. Whenever we try to manipulate nature's plan, as we sometimes arrogantly think we have the power to do, we only get ourselves in trouble and end up suffering from the consequences.

Retrospectively we see the folly in which the traditional medicine model tried to cure our bodies from the outside. We need only to reflect on what was done in the past in the name of science, medicine, and health. I can recall my childhood friends getting their tonsils removed because they were thought to be unnecessary. Also, appendixes were removed many times for no other reason than that they were there. This was especially true for females undergoing any type of abdominal surgery; in the past, a large percentage of hysterectomies performed resulted in the removal of the appendix. Before my time there was bloodletting, mercury poisoning, the frontal lobotomy, and so on. My concern is not what went on in the past, but rather what are we doing today that will cause our grandchildren to wonder, "What in the world were they thinking?"

New Zealand researchers hypothesized in a 1997 issue of *Epidemiology* that "it is theoretically possible that immunization may contribute to the development of allergic disease." The study showed that those few children who were fortunate enough not to have their vaccines had not reported any incidence of asthma or allergies. Of the majority, the vaccinated children, 23 percent had episodes of asthma, and 30 percent had consultations for other allergic illness. The researchers concluded, "The findings presented here are consistent with the hypothesis that some component of infant immunization may increase the risk of developing asthma in childhood."[2] Again, we see an example of how trying to cure the body from the outside in can do harm to our bodies by decreasing its ability to heal on the inside.

As we mentioned in Chapter 2, there are certainly times that drugs and surgeries are not only necessary, but life-saving. In fact, I am grateful for having the best crisis-care doctors in the world a relatively short distance from where I live. We are not dismissing the need for crisis care. If you find yourself in a severe state of health, please listen to your health-care provider. Our prayer for you is that, as you move out of crisis care and into health, you adopt the Possibility lifestyle. By embracing a path of wholeness, you will reduce your susceptibility to sickness and the need for crisis care in the future.

Our bodies heal from the inside out. Healing is an innate internal process that always occurs in proportion to our expression of life or, if you will, our ability to function in an optimal way. Before there is disease, there is dys-function. The ability to express life then becomes our healing potential. Naturally, we have the ability to heal from any disease known to humankind. This should give us great hope in overcoming all types of illness.

The body is in a constant state of renewal and regeneration. Every cell in our body replicates itself in some God-given miraculous way. It has been said that the best care most doctors can give is to help release the doctor that resides inside. Acquired immunodeficiency syndrome (AIDS) has certainly taught us one thing—to help people with AIDS survive we need to build up their resilience on the inside. To combat every AIDS infection with antibiotics or to treat AIDS with chemotherapy after a person gets cancer is a very futile effort.

As a society, we have been so caught up in the artificial management of symptoms via high technology from the outside that we have forgotten about the supreme ability of our bodies to heal themselves on the inside. This is like limiting yourself to a life in a cave, substituting a dim flashlight for the brilliance of the sun. When faced with the decision to choose between humans' highest form of technological medical advances and God's seemingly simple health design, I will always choose God's. Human-made can never be as good as God-made. The Bible says, "But God hath chosen the foolish [simple] things of the world to confound the wise" (1 Cor. 1:27, KJV).

The wisdom that resides within our body is far greater than one can imagine. The body is processing data on a moment-by-moment basis. Sensing the subtle changes in the oxygen levels in the air, temperature variations, and blood-sugar swings and making unnoticeable metabolic alterations in our physiology, we can continue to function at optimal levels, even in less than optimal environments. The body has an unbelievable surveillance mechanism, allowing the immune system to find and destroy any invading germs or atypical cells before they can grow and reproduce themselves into infections, tumors, and cancers. We have an immune system constantly protecting our bodies from any foreign invaders that may jeopardize our health. All we have to do is not get in the way of this highly balanced system.

In many ways, health is very similar to grace. Health isn't something we need to go out and get. It is inherent within us all. It is a free gift. When our systems are free to function the way God designed, we can get well and stay well. The wisdom of the body is the doctor within, on the job every day and every hour, constantly working to heal, repair, and regenerate. Our job is to remove any blockages that may interfere with the communication between the producer and the product (mind–nerve–body), keep the product clean of excess toxicity, and provide the basic component parts (nutrition) for cellular regeneration. The next chapter looks more closely at having a healthy diet and fit lifestyle. Eating right and keeping fit help your body stay healthy so that you can live A.D.I.O.

YOUR SOUL: EXPERIENCE GOD'S LOVE BY LIVING A.D.I.O.

To get connected to the Source is to be filled with our heavenly Father's love from *above*. St. John has been called the apostle of love. The gospel and letters he wrote in the New Testament speak of love more than seventy times. It has been said that when he was asked to speak to those eager to hear his words, he would simply say, "God is love."

When people are unhappy, they often try to make up for it with things like money, drugs, alcohol, or even work or relationships. Many of our obsessive behaviors are attempts to achieve a substitute from the outside for what is lacking or insufficient on the inside. The truth is that our need for material things betrays our deep, inner, spiritual lack of love. The paradox in my life was that I was blessed with all the material things again later in life. Now being fulfilled on the inside helps me to really appreciate everything else in life. In other words, happiness or genuine joy originates from *above*, comes *down* through God's Son, and resides *inside* of me. Then *out* of me flows love and joy.

Throughout the years in my practice, as I matured in my spiritual walk, I would often see physical dis-eases and emotional maladies that were directly related to spiritual disconnectedness or brokenness. The first dis-ease noted in the Bible was when Adam felt naked and ran in fear. The opposite of love is not hate, but fear. Many people have serious physical and emotional issues as a result of living in fear.

One of the most common stresses on our souls is fear. We worry about what we fear. Think of what you worry most about—events that may occur sometime in the future. It is perfectly normal to be afraid in the midst of a fearful event, being mugged, for example. But we spend inordinate amounts of time fearing things that may or may not come to pass in the future. For example, if you get bad news, say from a medical pathologist, your fear is of the future and what it will hold for you.

But love overcomes fear. One of my favorite scriptures, which beautifully illustrates the A.D.I.O. principle and its direct contradiction to fear, comes from the book of John. There Jesus said: "I tell you the truth, the Son can do nothing by himself; he can do only what he sees his Father doing, because whatever the Father does the Son also does. For the Father loves the Son and shows him all he does" (John 5:19–20, NIV). We see from this scripture that our heavenly Father loves us and shows us what he is doing and therefore what we should do *(above down)*. Then Jesus does whatever the Father leads him to do, and this forms the model of his divine purpose for our lives *(inside out)*. Walking by faith in love is inversely proportional to fear. To the degree we can walk in faith and live only in the present in any given situation, we will experience diminishing fear.

Love occurs in the now. John writes, "Dear friends, let us love one another, for love comes from God. Everyone who loves has been born of God and knows God" (1 John 4:7, NIV). God has given us the amazing gift of being able to choose to allow the very God who controls the universe and holds all things together, who heals all our diseases, to live in us and fill us with his perfect love.

Our decision to receive God's love, and through that abundance of his perfect love to love others, is the vital key to all healing. The apostle John goes on to say, "There is no fear in love. But perfect love drives out fear because fear has to do with punishment. The one who fears is not made perfect in love" (1 John 4:18). Living A.D.I.O. frees us from fear. Love is the great equalizer in the stresses, trials, and tribulations of life.

Love has healing power for our souls. In my practice, I attempt to see God at work in every patient's life. From a perspective of loving care, God's Spirit helps me to view my patients with his compassion. Sometimes if a fearful or anxious thought comes to me, I say a silent prayer asking the Holy Spirit to fill me again with his presence, so that everyone whom God divinely appoints to be in our office that day can experience the healing power and loving touch of God.

Adopting his perspective has released me from the tremendous stress of trying to perform as a doctor. People come in and experience the Father's love through me in a very significant spiritual, healing way. Often my patients confide in me at the conclusion of their consultation time, "I don't know why, but I already feel better." I have yet to do anything to them physically, but I have already started to care for them in a spiritual sense, with an intent that they feel God's love and receive healing. Our patients often tell me that when they enter our office, they physically feel love. Our staff knows God, and we make it a priority to create an environment of love. When patients are on a healing journey, receiving love and compassion are absolutely essential; many times they are feeling this spiritual love for the first time.

The path toward healing usually begins in loving service toward others. I have heard my pastor and co-author, Dr. Robert A. Schuller, eloquently use the illustration of the Dead Sea.. He describes the Dead Sea as having an inflow with no outflow. The Dead Sea is called the Dead Sea because it has no life.

To avoid becoming like the Dead Sea in our lives, we must have an inflow of love. Then we need to express this love to all those God puts in our path. To be of service to others enables us to experience freedom. As we give freely, we become a vessel through which an ever increasing volume of love flows. The more love that flows into and through us, the greater the healing capacity we have. The more we give, the more we receive. Love is an *inside* spiritual experience that flows *out* of us to others.

As Dr. Candace Pert explains in her book *The Molecules of Emotion*, when we "feel" love, every cell in our body experiences love chemicals through what are called neuropeptides.[3] This means not only is our immune system in love, but so are the cells in our spleen, our liver, and every other vital organ in our body. That is why we can viscerally feel love. Love and our other emotions are not just "feelings," but are literally neurochemicals that physically exist in our bodies. When we choose to feel hatred, resentment, or fear, all of our tissues begin to get bathed in the toxic neurochemicals associated with those feelings.

Once again love is a choice. Unquestionably, love has a very positive, healing effect on our body. When you choose love, you choose to be bathed on the inside with miraculous healing neurochemicals. As we choose love, we heal from the inside, and we then create the unlimited capacity to share this healing love with others. Love then becomes a way of life. The way of love becomes easy when we appreciate that God loves us, just as we are, in all of our brokenness.

YOUR SPIRIT: STAY CONNECTED TO GOD BY LIVING A.D.I.O.

B. J. Palmer wrote about the connection to the Source in many of his writings. He said there were many frequencies in the airwaves; it was up to us to choose the frequency we want to tune into. He called the frequency he tuned to "radio station G.O.D." To tune into station G.O.D. is to live an inspired life.[4] To have spiritual guidance from God in all aspects of our life is a very uplifting way to live.

In 1986 just after I left a group practice to start my own in a building my dad owned, I was very excited with all that went into starting fresh. And moving into my dad's building also eased my fear of failure. All the circumstances seemed to be perfect. After about a year, however, I grew uncomfortable with where I was practicing. The longer I stayed there, the more locked into the situation I felt. I began to dread going in the office. I loved all of my patients, but I was sensing a call to practice in another city.

During that time my wife and I had purchased a new home. We scraped together everything we had just to come up with the minimal down payment, unaware of all the expensive extras we needed like landscaping, new flooring, window coverings, appliances, and all of the other incidentals that go with moving from a very small condominium to a four-bedroom house.

Although on the surface I appeared successful, I began to lose the excitement of building my practice. I was even losing interest in chiropractic. The very art that had saved my life now drained my life. I had committed my life to God through the service of helping others with chiropractic, but now that commitment was waning. I began to spend more nights on the couch watching late movies because I was unable to sleep. Something was wrong, and I needed to change. But we were deep in financial commitments.

Then some very interesting circumstances began to occur in my life. One day when my wife and I were attending the Crystal Cathedral, my wife decided to purchase a *Possibility Thinkers' Bible*. I took it home that night and began to read. For the first time, God's immutable truths began to jump off the page for me. I began to grow in my personal relationship with God, and I realized what it meant to be in relational intimacy with God. I asked Jesus not only to be my Savior, which he had been for years, but also to be the Lord of every aspect of my life.

I began a journey of trusting God in guiding and directing my life. I began to hear his "still small voice" speak to my life. At first, I relied on

God's voice for some of my lesser important decisions. Interestingly, I kept getting the "feeling" I needed to move on in my career in spite of my limited finances. One Sunday morning, Dr. Robert H. Schuller talked about making those tough decisions that seem at the moment impossible; he talked about dreaming big dreams, about risk and fear. He revealed that the worst decision is never to even try.

I felt like God was directing his message at me. Then I found myself in one of those can't-get-to-sleep nights. Then this nudging began to occur, until I felt like I was physically kicked out of bed. I finally got out of bed at 3:30 A.M. The urge to change the direction of my life was so strong that I needed to talk to my wife that very moment. I had to ask her how she felt about my pressing life crisis.

I needed her permission before I risked our house and all that we had worked for, because I heard God's voice leading us in a new direction. I woke my wife up and asked her if we could go for a walk. We walked to a park bench inside a gazebo, next to a beautiful moonlit lake. I explained to her that I was unhappy and my enthusiasm was gone in the current situation. I told her I wanted to start over again, felt God was directing me to build a practice somewhere in our neighborhood. This meant I would move out of the building my dad owned and forgo the sense of security that gave me.

I asked for her understanding; she gave me comfort. I asked for her thoughts; she gave me encouragement. I asked that she stick by me in this transition; she gave me a commitment unconditionally in love. That decision was tough, yet retrospectively it was one of the best decisions I have ever made.

Looking back on that now, I understand that the Holy Spirit was working in me for his pleasure and purpose. God's plans are always better than anything we could possibly come up with on our own. Like the advice we give our children, although it may not always feel good in the present, in the end we only want what is best for them. The Heavenly Father who loves us wants only the best for us. He is a good God. He wants to guide us primarily through the Holy Spirit toward an abundantly rich life. He doesn't punish us in illness or in life's circumstances.

Yes, we do reap what we sow. If we live a life contrary to what is best, it is not God who "gets us." There will always be consequences of our actions, due to natural law. If we drink excessively, we cannot blame God if we lose job, family, or good health. God gives us the freedom to make choices. In those choices he still loves us in an unconditional way. If we listen to the Father's voice, he will see us through every situation.

Ask God's Spirit in all ways to direct your life. Imagine having a personal consultant who knows eternity past and eternity present. This consultant always knows what is best for us and loves us unconditionally beyond human capacity or understanding. This mighty counselor can direct not only our affairs, but also the affairs of the entire universe. We can tap into his wisdom anytime. In fact, he loves for us to give him all of our concerns and worries. We simply need to tune in to his wisdom and guidance.

Allow your spirit to tune in to God. We have the freedom to choose the frequency we want to be "connected" to in life. We can listen to radio station G.O.D. or to W.I.I.F.M. — the "what's in it for me" station, which puts the focus on self-centeredness. In the W.I.I.F.M. mode, we tend to focus on our limitations. We see our challenging circumstances rather than our abundant blessings. If the circumstance does not appear to be good, we tend to blame God. This process begins in resentment and moves toward spiritual disconnectedness. Spiritual disconnection blocks us from receiving the deepest kind of life-giving love. As the Scriptures say, "A heart at peace gives life to the body" (Prov. 14:30). Inner turmoil sets us up for many psychological illnesses as well as physical maladies.

When our life is controlled by things and situations outside of ourselves, we live "outside in," instead of A.D.I.O. Jesus described how A.D.I.O. happens spiritually in John 16:7, "But I tell you the truth: It is for your good that I am going away. Unless I go away, the Counselor will not come to you; but if I go, I will send him to you."

Before the indwelling of the Holy Spirit, the disciples had a God on the outside looking in, but after receiving the Spirit *above*, who came *down* to dwell *inside*, they had God's presence on the inside, working his purposes though them and *out* to the world.

Jesus also revealed, "I have much more to say to you, more than you can now bear. But when he, the Spirit of truth, comes, he will guide you into all truth" (John 16:12–13). Jesus is teaching us two exceptional truths:

1. He says that he has more to say to us, but in the natural physical realm, we can't hear what God wants to tell us. In order for us to understand the more profound, yet more real, spiritual realm, we need to be in the Spirit and therefore have the Spirit in us.

2. By his Spirit, Jesus is willing to partner with us in all aspects of our lives in a supernatural way. His promise here is that he will guide us in the truth. This would be like having Albert Einstein as our teacher for basic math. As we have heard so many times, "Then you will know the truth, and the truth will set you free" (John 8:32).

Possibility Living is living A.D.I.O. We are free from the bondage of the world's limitations, whether mental, spiritual, or physical enslavement. Teacher and founder of the Vineyard movement, John Wimber often used the phrase "naturally supernatural." We see the world not through our limited natural senses, but through a spiritual lens or perspective. A.D.I.O. is seeing reality from God's perspective instead of our own. Human knowledge and experience produce a natural perspective, but supernaturally we can see life through God's Spirit of wisdom.

Possibility Living that's lived *above, down, inside, out* allows us to

- tap into those gifts that God has promised for us;
- experience supernatural peace, which cannot come from circumstances, but from God's grace power and mercy;

- appreciate those divine appointments with people. There are no coincidences. God can and does supernaturally intervene much more than we could ever begin to understand this side of heaven;

- call on this supernatural power to strengthen us in times of need. Living naturally supernaturally eliminates most of our struggles and anxieties;

- live in the present free from the shackles of fear, worry, guilt, and resentment.

Imagine living without all that psychological baggage most of us carry with us. To experience peace, we must live in the present moment. The Scriptures advise us to give up the baggage; it is an unnecessary load. "Take my yoke upon you and learn from me, for I am gentle and humble in heart, and you will find rest for your souls. For my yoke is easy and my burden is light" (Matt. 11:29–30).

When we learn to receive this spiritual love from above, we have an unlimited abundance for others. As we open up the channel for this complete love, we have the resiliency, power, and strength to love and to be compassionate, purposeful human beings.

GOD'S A.D.I.O. PLAN FOR US IS GOOD!

The Father *above* wants to come *down* and dwell *inside* of you so that you have the strength and power to live *out* all of his possibilities for you. He wants to be a partner in your business, marriage, child rearing, and even recreation. All he asks is that we love him first, then those around us. God says it all here, when he says: "For I know the plans I have for you, declares the Lord, plans to prosper you and not to harm you, plans to give you hope and a future. Then you will call upon me and come and pray to me, and I will listen to you. You will seek me and find me when you seek me with all your heart" (Jer. 29:11–13).

We are to be thankful for all that we have in every situation. This has been called an attitude of gratitude. When we get connected to the

Source, we have hope, because when we walk in the Spirit, we are promised a plan of prosperity. All we have to do is seek him first.

God doesn't want robots; he wants us to make a decision for him and his love. What makes love special is that it is freely given without an expectation of being returned.

Possibility Living relies upon God *above*, by His Spirit to come *down* to us, and by our invitation to dwell *inside* us, so that he might flow *out* of us, not only for our eternal salvation, but for all aspects of our daily lives now, including our relationships, careers, and health. He is in control. We live the Possibility life when we seek his spiritual light in the form of love, peace, power, and guidance *(above down)*. God's word in our lives guides us in the way we are to live: "Your word is a lamp to my feet and a light for my path" (Ps. 119:105).

We then become empowered to be beacons of light and to share hope. His light within us shines through us to encourage others. As Jesus instructs, "You are the light of the world. A city on a hill cannot be hidden. Neither do people light a lamp and put it under a bowl. Instead they put it on its stand, and it gives light to everyone in the house. In the same way, let your light shine before men, that they may see your good deeds and praise your Father in heaven" (Matt. 5:14–16, NIV).

CHAPTER 5

CHOOSE THE HEALING POWER OF TOUCH

Dr. Douglas Di Siena

God created us with the need to be touched and to touch. Possibility Living is filled with positive, affirming, and healing touch. Without it, life would be stripped of the tangible possibilities that come when we communicate by touch. I personally witnessed this inborn need for touch when my sister-in-law, Fabi, gave birth to her son Dominick.

Just after Fabi had given birth, the obstetrician briefly showed the baby to her and then handed him over to the neonatal nurse. The nurse evidently thought it was important to clean the baby before doing anything else. Next came a litany of procedures, none of which was necessary for his well-being, because the neonatalogist already checked over the baby's physical systems. Everything appeared healthy. Then the nurse began taking the baby's measurements—weight and length. It seemed to take an eternity, but the nurse stuck to her slow routine. She simply refused to give Fabi her baby back until all her tasks were completed.

In the meantime, Fabi was crying out with all of her remaining energy, "Please let me have my baby! Please let me have my baby!" As the tension rose, all of us insisted that the nurse put Dominick back into his mother's arms. Even the obstetrician and the other nurses, who graciously stayed after their shift just to comfort Fabi, requested that she finish whatever remaining work she had left after the mother had some time to touch and hold her baby.

I will never forget the heart-wrenching sight of my sister-in-law leaning over the side of her bed, with tubes attached to her and tears streaming down her fatigued face, asking for her precious baby. Her emotion swept over us all, as we all felt not only her desire, but also her absolutely profound need to touch her baby. At long last, the nurse finally handed the screaming baby to his mother. She seemed completely unconcerned about Fabi's or the baby's innate need for the completion of the birth process with the loving cuddling of Dominick in his mother's arms. The moment Fabi touched Dominick, the screaming subsided, the tears ebbed, and joyful love flowed from mother to son.

I also experienced the healing power of touch during my wife's first labor. We used a drugless natural birthing method called "Bradley." In this meditative method the expectant mother performs deep relaxed breathing, while the coach assists in keeping the mother completely relaxed. During her contractions, my wife, Mariela, would take deep breaths, relax, and meditate. My job was to help her stay completely calm. I would gently touch her tense muscles, reassure her, and, most important, love her. I was never so proud of my wife. Throughout her labor, no one could tell she was even having a contraction because she looked as if she were sleeping.

We were progressing through her labor nicely until an unexpected visitor interrupted our intimate time of touch. My wife was startled by the strange touch of this person's hand on her foot. For the first time, she felt labor pain. But when the visitor left and I began again stroking the area of pain, Mariela relaxed and her pain subsided. Through healing touch, I felt connected to my wife as never before.

POSSIBILITY LIVING INCLUDES HEALING TOUCH

Touch—it's essential to our well-being. Without exception, human beings require close intimate human contact. Touching is not optional. Rather, touching is an essential ingredient of the four A's of successful relationships in Possibility Living.

Loving touch can be demonstrated when we give the following:

- *Attention*. People need to be heard. We give our attention to those we love. Often we convey our attention by *touch*.

- *Acknowledgment*. People need to be recognized. We acknowledge the presence and the value to us of those we love. Just the slightest *touch* can acknowledge the presence of one you love. With your touch you are communicating, "I know you are here and your being here is important and special to me."

- *Affirmation*. People need to be understood. We affirm those we love. At times, the most personal way to communicate affirmation is through *touch*, like a hug or a squeeze on the arm or shoulder.

- *Affection*. People need to be loved. We often demonstrate affection most intimately to those we love with *touch*.

Healing touch embodies the concept of A.D.I.O. We are God's conduits of healing touch. From *above*, the Father comes *down* to us and lovingly touches us. As his touch fills us on the *inside* with love and joy, we reach *out* to touch others. As we explore the healing power of touch, we will see the need to be a conduit of God's love and compassion. Filled with his compassion, we can go forward and provide healing touch, which is only effective when given with the right intent. The right intent comes from A.D.I.O.

How do you focus your thoughts when you awaken each morning? Are you focused on outside issues or on God and getting connected to his love and direction? I check myself by taking an inventory of what I think about when I awake in the morning. One of my morning prayers is to be filled and renewed with his power and to be in tune with his agenda for my day. If we are to be effective in our laying on of the hands, then we must be spiritually connected. "And do not be conformed to this world, but be transformed by the renewing of your mind, that you may prove what the will of God is, that which is good and acceptable and perfect" (Rom. 12:2, NAS).

Touch, or the laying on of the hands, is one of the most biblically based, ancient forms of healing. The promise of Scripture is that we will lay hands on the sick and they will recover. We see that promise modeled in the life of Jesus.

JESUS' HEALING TOUCH

Before I survey a few of the scientific reports that demonstrate our need for touch, I will explore the spiritual validation for touch. Jesus modeled the importance of touch in his earthly ministry.

> Large crowds followed Jesus as he came down the mountainside. Suddenly, a man with leprosy approached Jesus. He knelt before him, worshiping. "Lord," the man said, "if you want to, you can make me well again." Jesus touched him. "I want to," he said. "Be healed!" And instantly the leprosy disappeared.
>
> Matthew 8:1–3

"The laying on of hands" is demonstrated many times in the teachings of Jesus. Touch was used biblically in healing and for blessing. It is interesting to note that when Jesus was in his hometown and was unable to perform any miracles because of the people's unbelief (Matt. 13:54–58), he still laid his hands on a few people and healed them. The laying on of the hands is so powerful that it can overcome a lack of faith. When Jesus appeared to the disciples after his resurrection, he promised that his followers would "place their hands on sick people, and they will get well" (Mark 16:18).

We see in the Scriptures that Jesus didn't just preach healing, he practiced it. "When the sun was setting, the people brought to Jesus *all* who had *various kinds of sickness*, and *laying his hands on each one, he healed them*" (Luke 4:40, emphasis added). Notice that this passage says Jesus healed *all*. It is in his will for us to be well and in his character to heal us.

A patient came to see me who was also under the care of an oncologist for a recurring thyroid cancer. Previously, she had been treated for cancer with chemotherapy, after which it had gone into remission. When her cancer reappeared, her oncologist left her with few choices. Her options were more chemotherapy or a radical surgery that would leave her grossly disfigured and impaired. Neither was promising. She decided to try "alternative care." I informed her that in our chiropractic center for wellness we did not treat any disease. That process should be left for her oncologist. The care we offered would free her of any blockages between her mind and her body that might be inhibiting her body's natural ability to heal itself.

We did our best as a team to remove all external and internal toxins. We also talked about spiritual issues. I made sure that with every adjustment, I was free to release whatever healing power God was sending through me A.D.I.O. One particular day, I came to a room that had the door closed. Most of the time our patients like to leave the door open. Our office is like a large family, and everybody gets to know everyone else rather quickly. As I approached the room, I read her name on the chart. Anticipating bad news, my heart began to sink. This patient had been in my prayers for a long time. I had stayed up many nights going over her case searching for what I might be missing or anything else I could be doing to facilitate her healing.

The most dreaded time in practice is when a person's health is not restored. I slowly opened the door and tried to read her expression. Tears were streaming down her face. I reached out to hold her hand. Refusing my hand, she stood up and gave me a hug. Sobbing and hugging, she whispered in my ear, "Praise God. I am healed."

Evidently, she felt I was the one needing comfort. She then described her cancer experience as a long nightmare from which you can't seem to wake up. Yet throughout her illness, she never lost faith in God. She was always positive, upbeat, and so appreciative of every time I laid my hands on her. With every adjustment she would say, "Thank you." In her gratitude she made my family a Christmas gift that we take out every year and set by our tree. Not only did God's healing touch flow through me to her, her hug brought comfort and healing to me as her doctor.

God's healing power surges through us as we touch others. As a doctor, I have seen healing touch at work. I often wonder what it would have been like to have lived with the Great Physician, Jesus. Being in close proximity with the Physician, soaking up every word he said, and seeing everything he did would have been awesome. At times I imagine what touching him might have felt like. Luke 6:17–19 reads, "A large crowd of his disciples was there and a great number of people from all over Judea, from Jerusalem, and from the coast of Tyre and Sidon, who had come to hear him and to be healed of their diseases. Those troubled by evil spirits were cured, and the people all tried to touch him, because power was coming from him and healing them all."

I love this passage because we begin to get just a glimpse of the immense power of Jesus. The word "power" comes from the Greek word *dunamis*. It means "a power residing within." All of us have access to God's power. His *dunamis* is A.D.I.O. This power flows freely from *above down* to us, comes *inside* us, and through us reaches *out* to others. Jesus desires for us to use his powerful healing touch. God's power creates our bodies, recreates our bodies, and ultimately is the only power that can heal our bodies.

Jesus clearly commands us to heal the sick, "Heal the sick, raise the dead, cure those with leprosy, and cast out demons. Give as freely as you have received!" (Matt. 10:8). He gives us this healing power as a free gift from above. We are to give away all that we have received, including his healing touch. As with any vessel, the more healing that flows out, the more that can come in.

When I walk into my office, I appreciate the precious gift and privilege to be able to lay my hands on many, many people every day. I truly believe that I am increasingly blessed as I increasingly give. We all can tap into this healing power. We are more or less effective in healing depending on our willingness to be obedient to God's will. Our job, especially for those who are called to heal, is to simply be responsible for the vessel. God takes care of the rest. That means living the A.D.I.O. purposeful life.

ARE YOU UNCOMFORTABLE WITH TOUCH?

Many people are uncomfortable with the idea of touch. A few of my patients have asked me if I am uncomfortable laying hands on so many people. Touching comes naturally to me, having been raised in an Italian home where touch in the form of hugs, kisses, and pats on the back was more common than a handshake. Handshakes involve limited touch. With hugs there is openness, a sharing, and a way to offer a deeper part of yourself.

This level of touch is also quite evident in my wife's family, who are from South America. It is customary in many parts of South America to kiss on the cheek as a form of greeting. In the United States things are different. I reflected on those cultures in which family and community were of utmost importance. Invariably, they all had touching, including hugs, as a common denominator.

When on a family vacation in Italy, I can recall the men gathering in the streets to play music and dance. They had barrels in which they were roasting chestnuts. Many of the women were also involved, yet most of them seemed to just enjoy watching their husbands sing and dance and carry on. I was amazed at this spectacle. My father asked in his best Italian if there was a particular celebration. There was none. They were just celebrating for the sheer love of life. Before we knew what was happening they had pulled my father in the circle, and he was singing the songs (as best he could) and dancing arm in arm with the rest of the men. I couldn't think of any better stress reduction—no Valium needed for these people, just some music, the smell of roasted chestnuts, and the atmosphere of love and community.

The healing power of touch has no cultural or ethnic boundaries and can be conveyed by anyone willing to love and serve. I believe that those of us who are "laying on hands" in healing vocations understand the importance of our attitude with respect to touch. This book, however, is primarily for those not in the "healing business." All of us touch people every day. If we can appreciate the power of loving and caring touch, we can go through our days with the intent to help and to serve while sharing God's healing love with all those we meet by divine appointment. Just imagine all of the opportunities we have to share our heavenly Father's love with healing touch. We can start with our spouse or loved one.

All people have a need and desire for the four A's: attention, acknowledgment, affirmation, and affection. Loving touch can demonstrate all four. Often a child's initial vision of God comes through his or her relationship with a parental figure. If there is an intense level of love at home, then a child can more easily grasp God's eternal love for him or her. Love unlocks our ability to touch one another and nonverbally say "I love you." Just like a picture, a touch is worth a thousand words.

My first priority in facilitating people's pathway of healing is to show them how to connect with God's love and awesome healing power through touch. Healing touch, appropriately given, is also needed in the workplace, at church, and in all of our relationships.

TOUCHING WITH THE INTENT TO HEAL

Increasing in popularity are those health-care professions that utilize touch as their primary means of healing. People have a need to be touched by their doctor or therapist. The most obvious reason why the "alternative" health-care professions have been booming is because they are very effective. Alternative practitioners typically provide a high-touch, noninvasive, low-risk, and low-cost service. Alternative professions for the most part aim to facilitate healing rather than provide a temporary cure.

Conversely, traditional health care has been relying on high-tech machinery. Beyond the crisis care of emergency medicine, patients need a loving, compassionate touch. Although machines are very valuable for life-threatening issues, machines lack the elements of relationship and touch so vitally important in matters of wellness and healing. Medical doctors, out of necessity, have become highly trained technicians relying more on machines and less on relating to their patients in a loving and caring way.

As a result of my miraculous healing from asthma, I have joined the multitudes of people who, after experiencing a profound restoration of health, feel the call to heal others as they have been healed. I believe that when people experience a momentous physical healing, the impact affects them emotionally as well as spiritually. This often leads the newly healed to involve themselves in the same health-care field in which they discovered healing. I have also noticed that many of those individuals believe that it was only by divine design that their lives turned around. Their way of giving back is to help the needlessly suffering by giving them a similar healing. These types of practitioners, lay or professional, touch with an intense desire for healing. They also have a greater level of compassion, because they have "been there" and understand the patient's need for touch.

I felt it was ordained for me to become a chiropractor. Since the age of seventeen, I have committed my life to serving God by serving others through chiropractic. I mention this to point out that, in order for healing touch to be effective, there must be strong intent or motivation toward healing on the part of the practitioner.

The intent behind the touch is critical. For example, in a study with neonatal nurses, one group of nurses stroked premature newborn babies with intent to help facilitate healing. The other group just went through the motions of stroking without any real care. The babies under the care of the nurses with the intent to heal did far better than those for whom the nurses lacked intent.[1]

My mentor often said that for a chiropractic adjustment to be all that it can be, it needs to be delivered with that "extra something special." That something is love. Whether it is the laying on of hands in a healing service, the chiropractic adjustment, or the stroking of a premature baby, if loving touch is done with a healing intent, it moves beyond the physical into the spiritual realm.

Although we may see sickness manifested in the physical, we are spiritual beings. For us to get completely well, it requires healing on a spiritual plane. All healing is an internal spiritual manifestation of God's awesome power. I believe that the laying on of hands delivers a transfer of energy that is just as real as the nerve energy we can see on an EEG. I envision an instrument being developed someday that can read this spiritual energy. In current studies in which people place their hands over a jar filled with distilled water, those subjects were able to repeatedly imprint radiation into the water.[2]

Healing touch has been validated in many recent research reports. At Duke University, scientists inadvertently discovered that rat pups separated from their mothers at birth had stunted growth, while those that remained with their mothers had normal growth. This was not due to any difference in nutrition between the two groups, because both groups had similar diets. Normally the mothers would touch their babies by licking them. This licking produced hormones necessary for growth and development.[3]

Researchers at the University of Miami have done studies on the effect of touch on premature babies. Premature babies spend the first part of their life separated from their family in an artificial, controlled environment. Obviously the touch that would normally occur when a mom cuddles with her baby is very restricted. Researchers demonstrated that when the premature babies were simply stroked by a mother, they had a 47 percent increase in body weight compared to similar infants who did not have the benefit of touch. The babies who were touched also showed enhanced development, perhaps as a result of quicker development of the nervous system.[4]

Another interesting study on the effectiveness of therapeutic touch was done by Daniel Wirth, M.S., J.D., president of Healing Sciences International, in Orinda, California. In a study using college students, he purposely inflicted small wounds in the students' arms. The students then stuck their arms through armholes in a partition. On the other side, some of the students' arms received therapeutic touch, while others did not. Those receiving therapeutic touch demonstrated a quicker healing response. When Dr. Wirth repeated the study, he and his colleagues had similar findings.[5]

So here's the bottom line: *touching with loving intent has healing power.*

THE IMPORTANCE OF BEING REFILLED

One of the lessons I am just beginning to learn about the laying on of hands is that we do need to be refilled. In Scripture we see Jesus going off by himself to be in prayer and communion with his Father. He knew that to give, he needed time alone with the Father to receive. Jesus lived a life for us all to model.

When I read Scripture and find that the words seem to be intended just for me, I am amazed. One of the issues that often arises in my relationship with my wife is my overcommitment to my practice. I believe I am doing God's will for my life. It is fulfilling for me to lay hands on people and watch the amazing healing power that resides within us all work.

Unfortunately, I sometimes overstep my work boundaries at the expense of my family and my body. Reality sets in when I read in the Scriptures: "And after He had sent the multitudes away, He went up to the mountain by Himself to pray; and when it was evening, He was there alone" (Matt. 14:23, NAS). Again, "Very early in the morning, while it was still dark, Jesus got up, left the house and went off to a solitary place, where he prayed. Simon and his companions went to look for him, and when they found him, they exclaimed: 'Everyone is looking for you!'" (Mark 1:35–37).

Jesus retreated from the multitudes to the mountain to be alone and have fellowship with the Father. In our current vernacular, we might say that Jesus needed "to have his batteries recharged." At one point, I pictured Jesus running around laying hands on everybody, healing everybody, feeding everybody, and preaching to and teaching everybody all of the time. But if Jesus, God's son, needed his batteries recharged, who did I think I was? I had forgotten the *above down* part of the A.D.I.O. formula.

Healing comes from above. Our power to lay hands on people comes from above. Healing is for God and by God. Certainly when Jesus left the multitudes, he had to leave behind someone who had been suffering, sick, or in need of him in some way. In doing so he revealed to us where his priorities lay. His first priority was the Father, then himself, then others. Jesus was fully aware of his energy level and the need to refuel.

THE POWER OF TOUCH TO BLESS

Another important purpose of the ancient ritual of laying on hands was for giving a blessing. This is also an area in which our culture lacks the powerful customs of the past. According to the *Nelson's Illustrated Bible Dictionary* the definition of "bless" or "blessing" is: "The act of declaring, or wishing, God's favor and goodness upon others. The blessing is not only the good effect of words; it also has the power to bring them to pass. In the Bible, important persons blessed those with less power or influence. The patriarchs pronounced benefits upon their children, often near their own deaths (Gen. 49:1–28)."[6]

I would have loved to have been one of the children Jesus took into his arms and blessed as recorded in the book of Matthew: "Then little children were brought to Jesus for him to place his hands on them and pray for them. But the disciples rebuked those who brought them. Jesus said, 'Let the little children come to me, and do not hinder them, for the kingdom of heaven belongs to such as these'" (Matt. 19:13–14, NIV).

THE HEALING TOUCH OF ANOINTING WITH OIL

Anointing with oil is another form of demonstrating God's healing power and blessings. We read in the Scriptures: "Is any one of you sick? He should call the elders of the church to pray over him and anoint him with oil in the name of the Lord" (James 5:14). To anoint is to apply oil to a thing or a person. This was a very common practice in the ancient Near East. Anointing was done for sacred, ordinary, or healing purposes.

In the above scripture, we are commanded to touch or anoint a sick individual with oil. Here we have the power of touch at work. We are told to call up the elders and pray. When we pray we are ultimately seeking God's will. Remember it is in God's will and his character to heal us. So when we seek him in prayer, to do his will, God will empower us for his purposes. We will explore more deeply Chapter 7 how the power of prayer helps us live life filled with God's possibilities.

When people are praying and believing in God's ability to heal, they become vessels of God's healing power. The early Christians realized that the power to heal was never from them, but from God above. They lived the A.D.I.O. principle. "Laying on hands" is one of the clearest examples of this principle.

It is our prayer that our readers have an opportunity to receive the laying on of hands, not as a result of sickness necessarily, but as a function of wellness. Laying on of hands is clearly scriptural as well as scientifically proven to have a very positive influence on our overall health and well-being. There are many ways to receive the healing effects of healing touch, through a professional such as a pastor or rabbi, chiropractor, massage therapist, nurse, or medical doctor or just a loving spouse or close friend. All have the ability to provide a healing touch when the intent to deliver God's healing power is present.

TOUCH OTHERS WITH GOD'S HEALING TOUCH

We also encourage you to provide healing touch to your loved ones as well as those in need. No degree is required to extend God's healing power. What's needed is simply a belief in God, a compassion for the sick, and the willingness to be used by God in service of others.

Possibility Living is filled with loving touch that intends to communicate God's love and healing power for everyone all of the time. As we touch others, not only will they be touched by God's healing power, we will be touched as well. And at times, the greatest healing comes to those who put aside their own brokenness in order to touch and help heal the brokenness in others.

CHAPTER 6

CHOOSE A HEALTHY DIET AND FIT LIFESTYLE

Dr. Douglas Di Siena

Possibility Living means making the right choices about health. By investing in your wellness, you will enjoy the many benefits of a healthy lifestyle. When it comes to a healthy diet and lifestyle, all the intention in the world without action will not be of any benefit. God's health plan requires action.

A healthy diet is not a program for weight loss. Although taking off weight may be the end result, eating right is a lifestyle, not a diet plan. Later in this chapter we will outline a simple, healthy way to lose weight, but first we want to talk about lifestyle. Diets are usually short-term programs to take off pounds, but rarely are they effective for maintaining a healthy weight over the long term. Most people who diet put the weight they lose back on in just a few months.

Possibility Living guides you toward a life of good nutrition and fitness and will result in a possibility-filled, long, fully functional life. Here are ten simple steps.

STEP 1: EAT SUPERFOODS

Superfoods should be consumed as regularly as possible because they fight disease and strengthen the immune system. These foods contain substances your body requires for maintaining health and regeneration. Remember that your body is constantly under repair. What you put into your body is used to rebuild your body.

Cruciferous vegetables. Most vegetables that are deep in color tend to be extremely beneficial. Their color reveals that they contain phytonutrients, natural chemicals that are extremely beneficial to our wellness. Foods loaded with phytonutrients provide powerful natural substances to maximize your healing and regenerating potential. One group of vegetables, the cruciferous family, which includes broccoli, cauliflower, cabbage, brussels sprouts, kale, mustard, kohlrabi, rutabaga, turnips, and radishes, is particularly valuable.

1. Cruciferous vegetables have been shown to aid in the prevention of breast and ovarian cancer.[1]

2. Sulforaphane is another phytonutrient found in cruciferous vegetables.[2] Sulforaphane has been shown to help in the removal of toxins and carcinogens (cancer-causing agents).[3]

Garlic. My mother asserted that garlic was good for everything that "ails you." It interesting to note which foods the Hebrews complained that they missed from Egypt. Numbers 11:5 says, "We remember the fish, which we used to eat free in Egypt, the cucumbers and the melons and the leeks and the onions and the garlic." The foods they missed were all extremely healthy. Leeks, onions, and garlic all have allyl sulfides, chemicals helpful in reducing cardiovascular disease (since garlic can thin the blood, talk to your doctor if you are on any blood-thinning drug). Garlic helps to support immune system function, while reducing the incidence of certain cancers.[4] Through this scripture, we can get a glimpse of the healthy diet God's people ate. It must have been God-inspired.

Tomatoes. Tomatoes are another superfood. Tomatoes have that bright color, which indicates richness in phytonutrients, specifically the carotenoid lycopene. Although beta-carotene gets the most positive press as a strong antioxidant, lycopene has twice its ability to fight free radicals. Antioxidants help the body fight against the formation of free radicals, which are atoms or groups of atoms that can damage cells, impair the immune system, and lead to infections and various diseases such as cancer and heart disease. Consuming foods that contain lycopene may help in the reduction of gastrointestinal cancers, as well as prostate cancer.[5, 6] Lycopene is also found in high concentrations in apricots, red grapefruit, and watermelon (grapefruit is one of my favorite foods—low-glycemic fruit high in fiber).

Leafy greens. Green leafy vegetables are another one of those neces-sary foods. They include kale, turnip greens, cilantro, spinach, parsley, endive, romaine lettuce to name a few. I try to have leafy vegetables twice a day, preferably raw. Greens have an abundant supply of two carotenoids, lutein and zeaxanthin. These may help age-related eye disorders such as macular degeneration. In addition, they also tend to have very high levels of folate, fiber, vitamin C, and beta-carotene.[7]

Soybeans. Soybeans seem to be one of those perfect foods. An excellent source of protein, soybeans are a plant and that means no cholesterol. Soybeans also have a type of phytonutrient known as phy-toestrogen, as well as having very strong antioxidant properties. Phytoestrogen may help explain the lowered incidence of cancer in countries where soy is regularly consumed. Phytoestrogen seems to have a protective effect against hormone-related cancers, such as breast and prostate cancer, and diseases like osteoporosis and heart disease. Soy may help reduce the incidence of menopausal symptoms as well as reduce the risk of other hormone-related problems.

A number of soy products are available to you as a super protein source. They include the following:

tofu

soy milk

soy flour

miso

soy protein

tempeh

Bee Pollen. Although not a lot of research has been done on the value of bee pollen, we do know it is loaded with phytonutrients and other substances we may someday begin to understand. The preliminary research has been very promising. Maybe more important than future research, however, is how people respond when they regularly consume bee pollen. In our experience, people who consume bee pollen seem to have an increased ability to regulate their sugar levels. They have less afternoon fatigue and a noticeable increase in workout strength and stamina.

STEP 2: INCREASE YOUR METABOLIC RATE

Our metabolic rate is the rate at which we burn calories. Obviously, the higher the rate, the greater the weight loss. The easiest and safest ways to increase our metabolism are through adequate caloric consumption and exercise by aerobic and weight-resistance training.

By eating at regular intervals, the body perceives an abundance of food and therefore allows for maximum burning. It is like a fireplace with a roaring fire. With lots of wood and plenty of oxygen you will get a very hot and furious fire. The other benefit of eating more regularly is that when it is time to eat, our blood sugar is not quite so low, so we tend to eat less. When I was a kid, my mom would always tell us not to snack before dinner. Why? Because she knew that snacking would reduce our appetite. As adults, we somehow think this principle reverses with age. It doesn't.

We can also increase our metabolism by exercise. I recommend exercising enough to burn between 1,500 to 2,500 calories per week, depending on stress levels and other activities in the day. For instance, I did cement work one summer while on a break from college. I was burning in excess of 3,000 calories a day. When I returned to school, I was suddenly spending the better part of each day sitting at a desk and my required exercise time needed to go way up. To get an idea of the rate calories are burned:

Walking burns approximately 300 calories per hour.

Jogging burns approximately 600 calories per hour.

I know what you're thinking. An apple is about 80 calories—I will just cut out the apple and forget the exercise. Please read on—there are far more benefits to exercise than meet the eye.

Please remember that the crucial point is to keep the metabolism burning at full speed. The real benefit, in terms of burning calories, comes hours after the exercise. Although it may be true that one would have to walk for about one hour to burn a scant 300 calories, the great news is that, later on in the day sitting at the dinner table, the person who exercised continues to burn calories at a much higher rate than the sedentary person. The benefits of the exercise continue long after the actual time spent exercising. If the benefit of exercise for the purposes of losing weight is not enough motivation to get you off of the couch, please see our list of the many benefits of exercise later on in this chapter.

STEP 3: AVOID CALORIES THAT HAVE NO NUTRITIONAL VALUE

Overly processed foods in general have less nutritional value and should be avoided. The first clue to processing is the color. A simple rule is to avoid foods, especially grains, that are white. White foods in general are either highly processed or have a very high starch content (both of which cause a very rapid rise in blood sugar levels).

The biggest culprits are white sugar and white grains (white breads, pastas, and rice). The bulk of our diet should be in the form of nutrient-dense greens and not grains; think *green*, not *grain*. Most of the nutrients and the fiber in the grain are in the outer portion or in the germ, which are removed in processing. When eating grains, choose the whole food.

Most meals customarily include a vegetable, protein, and a starch. A simple rule to a healthier diet is to double the vegetable portion in place of the starch. You will end up with a plate of food with more vitamins, minerals, and fiber. Another source of "empty calories" — calories with little or no nutritional value — are sodas, beer, and mixed alcoholic beverages. Water has no calories, can be flavored with citrus, and is an incredible cleansing agent. Far too many people walk around dehydrated and need to drink at least eight to ten glasses of water each day. Dehydration is a cause of toxicity. Have a glass of water available at all times. By the way, coffee, alcoholic beverages, and sodas don't count in your water intake.

Avoid foods that contain molds or mold toxins. Foods that go bad usually smell. That is why God put our nose right above our mouth. Always smell the food you are about to put in your body. If something does not smell good, do not eat it. One of the more serious toxins from mold is called aflatoxin, but it is one that is tough to completely eliminate from our diets. It is found mostly in commercial baked breads, cereals, and other grains. A lot of other foods that can contain toxic molds, such as fruits and vegetables, can be cleaned and made healthy with a thorough wash. Always wash your fruits and vegetables. Nuts can have toxic molds as well. This is why nuts should always be refrigerated, where it is cool and dry. Molds love moisture and warmth.

Commercially available bread should be toasted before consumption or kept in the freezer. In the book *The Cure for All Diseases*, Dr. Hulda Clark states that she tested baked goods found in local bakeries and they seem to be free of mold for the most part. With commercial breads, which are wrapped in plastic shortly after baking, the moisture gets sealed into the package and this creates the right environment for mold. She recommends baking your own bread and putting a little vitamin C in the mix. This keeps the bread mold-free for a longer time.[8]

STEP 4: KEEP YOUR BLOOD-SUGAR LEVELS RELATIVELY CONSTANT

Blood-sugar swings can cause weight gain as well as many kinds of toxicity issues for our body. When our blood sugar rises too high, our body releases insulin, which results in sugar getting stored as fat. Conversely, when our blood sugar goes too low, causing hypoglycemia, it creates a craving for sweets or sugary, simple-carbohydrate (high-glycemic) foods, even though the body does not need additional calories.

There are many ways to control blood sugar. To adequately understand blood sugar, you would need volumes of information, but we will try to simplify it here. The body does not tolerate high blood-sugar levels. In fact, high levels of sugar in the blood are very toxic, especially to the nervous system. For this reason, the nervous system protects itself by closely monitoring the blood sugar. When it becomes too high, it signals the pancreas to begin the process of producing insulin, which does not stop until the sugar levels are back to normal—or in many cases, until the blood sugar is below normal, producing hypoglycemia.

The role of insulin is to drive sugar from the blood into the tissue. Sugar goes into what are called glycogen stores (and only if they were depleted by recent exercise), which are located in both the liver and the muscle tissues. Whatever sugars are left over are then stored as fat. The take-home lesson here is: it is not just eating excess fat that makes you fat, but also the production of insulin, which lowers the high blood-sugar level by ultimately storing sugar as fat. The danger of replacing fatty foods with nonfat ones that are simple carbohydrates (high-glycemic foods) is that it results in continued weight gain.

When our blood sugar is driven too low in the form of hypoglycemia, our brain signals us to eat sugar in an attempt to bring up sugar levels. This is why after a very indulgent meal, we very often crave sweets or caffeine, both of which function to raise blood-sugar levels. One way to know if you have hypoglycemic problems is if you get tired or sleepy after a meal.

The glycemic index. With respect to blood sugar, different foods cause the body to react in different ways. Let us examine two different breakfast scenarios: I eat oatmeal with some protein and you eat the same amount of calories in the form of a plain white-flour bagel. Assuming we were both rested and not in glycogen depletion, your blood sugar would rapidly rise, followed by a surge in the release of insulin, effectively bringing blood sugars down and storing fat. Ultimately, you would have a lower blood-sugar level than when you first ate and the sugar you consumed would be stored as fat. You would experience a short-term burst of energy, followed quickly by a feeling of hunger. This is not because your body needs more food, but because your blood sugar is low. I, on the other hand, would notice a sustained energy surge. I would continue to have energy for at least three and possibly up to six hours after the meal.

When we eat a high-glycemic meal, we gain weight in three ways:

1. Insulin is released, driving the sugar into the tissue as stored fat.

2. Next we feel an artificial hunger in a relatively short period of time, urging us to eat unnecessary calories.

3. When our blood sugar drops, we tend to crave foods that provide a quicker energy surge; those foods are the high-glycemic, sugar foods that start the whole cycle all over again.

Foods with the lowest glycemic index are the best foods for weight control and blood-sugar stabilization. These types of foods do not break down as quickly and thus release their energy at a much slower rate. Foods will have a low glycemic index if they contain fiber, fat, or protein. Hence, whole foods will always be better for you. However, even whole foods have different indexes. For example, a banana has a much higher index than a strawberry, and carrots are much higher than asparagus. Most diabetic handbooks have a complete list of foods and their relative indexes.

Artificial sweeteners. Artificial sweeteners are another group of chemicals to be avoided. As with fat, when you need to have something sweet, always go natural first. There is considerable talk about the toxicity of artificial sweeteners. One sweetener had a cancer warning on it. Another has been reported as having serious side effects and, when heated, causing symptoms mimicking multiple sclerosis and lupus, headaches, and other neurological problems. The point is, food made in some chemistry lab does not belong in your body. Pass on those little packages, and go natural.

The following priority list will help when choosing a sweetener:

CHOICE OF SWEETENERS

1. stevia . . . first choice, use at will (Stevia, a South American herb, is reported to be 100–300 times sweeter than table sugar. It has no calories, and it is natural and nontoxic. Stevia can be purchased in the herbal section in most health food stores.)

2. honey

3. pure maple syrup

4. sucanat

5. fructose sugar

6. brown sugar

7. white sugar

8. artificial sweeteners . . . last choice, avoid if at all possible

Food combinations. You can take positive steps to reduce the insulin response to your meals so that your body will store less fat without restricting total calories. These steps will also keep the metabolism fully functioning and will enable your body to burn calories at a higher rate. As we mentioned above, foods that have fiber, good fat, or protein slow down the release of insulin. Therefore, if you do eat a starchy food with your meal, just make sure you have something with a large amount of fiber and/or some good (monounsaturated) fat. This will buffer the insulin response and give you less of a sugar swing.

If it is your goal to lose weight, remember that weight is not put on overnight, so do not try to lose it overnight. One of the keys to long-term weight management is to not starve your body. The body will respond by going into a famine mode, which I will talk about later in this chapter. This is why people who lose weight rapidly often gain back more weight than they took off. When they simply return to their previous caloric intake, their body grabs on to all of these calories and stores them as fat.

STEP 5: PREPARE FOOD IN HEALTHY WAYS

My list of the best-to-least healthy ways to prepare foods is as follows:

1. raw

2. steamed

3. stir-fried, wok-style

4. baked

5. broiled

6. barbecued, slow southern style, no smoke

7. microwaved

8. smoked

9. salted and pickled

10. deep-fried

Avoid making healthy food toxic. Although all types of cooking destroy vitamins and enzymes, microwaving may have an undesirable effect on the nutrient density of foods. Research demonstrates that when human breast milk is heated in a microwave, some of its ability to transfer immunity from mother to infant is destroyed. This not only diminishes the germ-fighting ability of the human breast milk, but, perhaps more important, it allows for the potential growth of harmful bacteria in the milk. If there were more research on microwave cooking, I imagine we might find additional hazards to our health.

Grilling or flame broiling is another way we can damage the foods we eat. Char, or flame, broiling creates many of the same carcinogens as are in cigarette smoke. Overcooking or blackening foods also has that carcinogenic effect. The same goes for fried foods—if you consume fried foods on a regular basis, you are increasing your intake of carcinogens. Dr. Victor E. Archer states that people who prefer to fry and flame-broil have a risk of pancreatic cancer thirteen times greater than those who cook their foods in other ways.[9]

STEP 6: ENJOY YOUR MEALS

Life should be enjoyed, and gathering around food is an opportunity for family, friends, and fellowship. The rule in our house is that we eat every dinner together at the table. To skip or avoid meals is to miss out on many celebrations and special moments. A meal can also be appreciated when one is alone. I have come to relish a quiet lunch when I can slow down, rest, and renew from my morning/afternoon appointments. I also use this quiet time for prayer and contemplation. This also allows me a time to be grateful for the bounty God has given me, as I pray a prayer of thanksgiving. While in this relaxed, almost meditative, state I find it much easier to take time to truly savor and enjoy every bite.

STEP 7: EXERCISE

Fitness is more important to your health than lean body mass.[10] In a study of just under 22,000 men, researchers found that lean but unfit men had double the risk of dying than lean, physically fit men. The really interesting part of this study is that unfit lean men had a higher mortality rate than did fit overweight men. Although exercise aids in weight loss, there are many other reasons to stay lean. There is no arguing that exercise improves longevity and quality of life.

A number of studies have demonstrated that exercise

- lowers cholesterol levels

- improves balance and coordination, even in the elderly

- strengthens bones

- fights insomnia

- reduces the effects of mental stress

- relieves depression

- helps control type II diabetes

- dissolves or prevents blood clots, possibly explaining exercise's protective effect against heart attacks

- decreases breast cancer risk by up to 60 percent

- cuts in half the risk of gastrointestinal bleeding in the elderly

- postpones many effects of aging

- increases resistance to infections[11]

For most of these studies, the key was not how much or how long you exercised, but simply the regularity.

- In a study performed by a team of Harvard University researchers who monitored 121,000 women, results showed that women who exercise as little as a half hour a day merely walking cut the incidence of colon cancer by 17 percent.[12] Those women who did engage in more strenuous workouts cut their risk of cancer by 50 percent.

- Duke University performed a study documenting the benefits that exercising as little as eight minutes a day had on clinical depression.

- Norwegian psychiatrist Egil Martinsen initiated an exercise program of one hour of aerobic exercise three times per week for forty-nine of his seriously depressed patients. Within thirty workouts, those who consistently exercised reported significant improvement in their depression. Consistent exercisers continued to be better off years later as well.[13]

Let us embrace things that are natural, have virtually no negative effects, and cost little or nothing—like exercise!

Before starting any exercise program, consult with a professional health-care provider. Different types of exercise are recommended for different people. There is no set standard for the best exercise. However, as a general rule, almost everyone should start slow, perhaps just walking or swimming.

The simple rule to keep in mind when exercising is to work up gradually to twenty minutes, preferably with an additional five-minute stretching warm-up and a five-minute cool-down time. Your heart rate should not exceed 60 percent of your maximum heart rate. It is important to remember that to burn fat, you need oxygen (the term "aerobic" means "with oxygen"). To ensure oxygenation, you need to monitor your heart rate and not allow it to get too high. To determine your maximum heart rate, subtract your age from 220. Then take 60 percent of that. This heart rate can be easily achieved by walking or even light bicycling.

Those more experienced can exercise for up to thirty minutes, not to exceed 80 percent of the maximum heart rate, with a goal of about 75 percent sustained maximum heart rate. Anything greater than 80 percent could cause an anaerobic state, which could lead to increased free radical damage. There should still be a five-minute warm-up and five-minute cool down with stretching.

STEP 8: MAINTAIN A HEALTHY WEIGHT

What about weight loss? Now that we have a general overview of what a healthy diet consists of, you may be concerned about a healthy way to lose weight. Most of us know that being overweight contributes to the big three: cancer, heart disease, and stroke. To be well for life, we should be appropriately lean for life.

The struggle with weight control seems to be epidemic, especially in advanced, technological cultures such as ours. In an attempt to lose weight, many people read popular diet books or emulate celebrities. Or worse yet, they go on a crash diet, starving the body not only of calories, but also of life-giving nutrition. When these quick-fix approaches don't work (and they don't), they resort to pharmaceuticals or surgery, an "outside-in" approach. Many "medical" approaches to weight loss have proven to be just as dangerous as being overweight.

I still have the ad from a major hospital listing the ten steps to wellness. One of the necessary steps for wellness was weight control. As a way to lose weight, it recommended a combination of two drugs and touted this drug combination as the safest yet, for both weight loss and curbing the appetite. This drug combination has since been removed from the market because of the extremely dangerous and potentially life-threatening side effects. My concern here is why should we jeopardize our health by risking dangerous and adverse side effects, when effective weight loss can be achieved in a very healthy way, without hunger, malnutrition, or any other sacrifice to health.

In fact, starvation actually promotes weight gain in the long run. Our bodies were created for survival. If the body senses a lack of food, the innate response is for it to become more efficient with every calorie it receives. For instance, back in the 1970s when we had the gas shortage, wouldn't it have been nice if our car became more fuel-efficient? Well, our body does just that. When the body perceives a famine, it utilizes whatever calories are consumed, and the moment there is any excess food, it is stored as fat for the future.

Some essential keys to healthy, sustained weight loss and weight management include the following:

- Eat mostly whole foods, deriving the main part of your diet from the plant kingdom.

- Do not eat excessively or to the point of being uncomfortable.

- Stay away from empty calories and avoid excess fats.

- Eat regular modest meals.

- Keep active and exercise regularly.

Slow and sure is the way to go. Besides, losing just 2 pounds per month is twenty-four pounds in a year.

STEP 9: MAKE SUPPLEMENTS PART OF YOUR DIET

Supplements—vitamins, enzymes, herbs, and minerals—should be a part of a regular healthy lifestyle to support the body's natural function for optimal wellness. Supplements should not be consumed only during sickness, nor should megadoses be taken. We should try to avoid the temptation of "treating" the body in an attempt to influence its physiology with things from the outside. If there is a medical condition that requires crisis care, then it may be appropriate to first try more natural remedies under the care of a qualified professional health-care provider.

Please see a health-care provider who works with nutrition on a regular basis for a personal consultation to determine your specific needs. If that is not possible, go to a reputable health food store and ask for a good—not the cheapest—multiple vitamin and mineral supplement.

Everyone needs a slightly different supplement regimen depending on dietary habits, stress levels, time spent working out per week, weight, and genetic factors. My program of daily antioxidants includes 20,000 IU of mixed carotenoids, 3 grams of vitamin C, 100 IU of vitamin E, and 200 micrograms of selenium. In addition, I recommend the entire B-vitamin family, minerals (they should be chelated for bioavailability), and one serving a day of "barley, super," or any other reputable brand powdered greens. There are certainly other herbs and natural substances that are helpful, but the above should indicate the fundamental content of a healthy nutrient supplement program.

Another issue here is the appropriate consumption of calcium for women. Studies have shown that when postmenopausal women supplement their diet with 1,000 milligrams of calcium, the result is a 43 percent reduction in bone loss.[14] Another important supplement in reducing bone loss is vitamin D; 400–800 units of D are recommended daily. Ipriflavones, a little-known but extremely crucial supplement for bone density, have been shown not only to inhibit bone reabsorption, but also to stimulate bone formation. Supplementation with up to 600 milligrams a day results in a significant increase in bone density in postmenopausal women who have already lost bone to the point of osteopenia or osteoporosis.[15]

STEP 10: A REQUIRED TIME FOR REST, RENEWAL, AND REGENERATION

Although we listed sleep as our 10th step, it is one of the most fundamental elements to a healthy and fit lifestyle. Studies have shown sleep deprivation to be a widespread health problem. A consistent lack of sleep seems to be responsible for decreased immune system function. Missing sleep also diminishes our ability to enter in the R.E.M. (rapid eye movement) sleep. People who lose R.E.M. sleep typically have low levels of seratonin levels, a brain neurotransmitter that in part regulates our mood. Low seratonin levels are likely to cause among other symptoms, fatigue and depression.

Emotional or physical stress is usually implicated as one of the most common causes of insomnia. Both of these issues are covered in upcoming chapters, especially in "Detoxify Your Stress" and "Detoxify Your Physiology."

In practice I have observed countless times when patients who complained of insomnia, or an inability to have a restful sleep, have been able to get a full and restful night of sleep after one chiropractic adjustment. My coauthor, Robert, has shared with me a similar experience. He explained, when he has restless nights, it is usually an indicator for him that he is in need of an adjustment, which allows him to return to normal sleeping patterns.

I challenge you not to forget this seemingly trivial, yet vital component to a healthy lifestyle. If you struggle with this issue, I believe the "Detox" chapters will give you the tools necessary to help you in this important step to Possibility Living.

EAT RIGHT AND BE FIT

This biblical text is my daily prayer for you. "Dear friend, I pray that you may enjoy good health and that all may go well with you, even as your soul is getting along well" (3 John 2, NIV). You may feel that maintaining a healthy diet and a fit lifestyle is too much to undertake at one time. We would like to remind you that the benefits will certainly be noticed and enjoyed in a relatively short time, while the unknown story (what won't happen as a result of this new healthy lifestyle) will benefit you for a lifetime.

Possibility Living puts the pieces together for making the whole puzzle of life a complete picture of living the way God intended—100 years with our eyes sharp and our bodies strong.

CHAPTER 7

CHOOSE
PRAYER

Dr. Robert A. Schuller

Prayer opens us up to hear God's voice and follow his plan for Possibility Living.

Through prayer we commune with God. More than just talking to God, communion is being with God. It is being in his presence—intimately knowing both his nature and character. Through prayer we acknowledge that he exists for us and believe that he can make a difference in our lives. Communing prayer allows God the opportunity to talk to us and us the time to listen to him.

Prayer can be practiced in a number of different ways. You can pray while driving to work, walking the dog, or resting in bed. It can be done on your knees, on your feet, or flat on your back. I have even heard that most skydivers pray while jumping from the plane. In other words, you can pray anytime and anyplace.

Some people pray silently. Others shout. I have been to a Korean church in which everyone prays aloud at the same time for about five minutes until an elder rings a bell signaling that it is time to stop. At the Wailing Wall in Jerusalem, many Jews chant their prayers while rocking back and forth. Others take their written prayers and stuff them into the cracks of the wall hoping to get closer to the holy seat of God. At the Blue Mosque in Istanbul, Turkey, I witnessed the Islamic prayers to Allah. After washing, Muslims lay down their rugs and prostrate themselves on the floor to show respect and honor to God.

Of the many different methods and ways of prayer, the one I like to follow was outlined by Jesus after his disciples asked him how to pray. In Luke 11:2–4, Jesus said:

Father, hallowed be thy name,
your kingdom come.
Give each day our daily bread.
Forgive us our sins;
for we also forgive everyone who sins against us.
And lead us not into temptation.

Most people recognize this as the basis of the Lord's Prayer. It forms a wonderful outline for praying and there have been many books written on praying according to it. Dr. Larry Lea, founder of the Church on the Rock, in Rockwall, Texas, teaches people how to pray for one hour straight every day following the outline of the Lord's Prayer.

There is no one way or method of prayer that is necessarily better than another. The important thing is to pray. Prayer is so important to Possibility Living that Scripture simply commands, "Pray without ceasing" (1 Thess. 5:17). Prepare your hearts and minds for a constant state of prayer, the kind St. Paul describes, so that your life is filled with the possibilities that come when you pray without ceasing.

OPEN UP TO GOD

After Jesus taught the disciples the Lord's Prayer, he taught them a parable about their need to come constantly and persistently before God in prayer. If we continue to reach out to him, God will not turn us away. He will fulfill our needs.

How is it possible to pray without ceasing? During the early Christian centuries, many became hermit monks who would not talk or socialize with anyone, devoting their lives completely to God and cutting themselves off from all society. Some lived on top of pillars. They survived only through the generosity of others who gave them portions of food and water. The pillar dwellers would lower a basket on a rope to the benevolent below and remain on top of their columns "free from the sins of the flesh."

Although there was a time in history when to pray without ceasing meant complete withdrawal from the world, I don't believe that is what God has in mind for us. We don't need to withdraw from life and isolate ourselves from others just to pray. God created us to be together. We see that from the beginning of creation.

As God created the world, he looked at what he had done each day and proclaimed, "It is good." He did this until he came to Adam. At that point he said, "It is not good." God was not pleased with Adam's solitary existence: "It is not good that man should live alone" (Gen. 2:18). Then God created Eve. Upon seeing them together, he said "It is very good."

This reminds me of an old joke about a conversation between Adam and God. God told Adam that he was going to create Eve. God said, "Adam, I'm going to create for you a partner who is beautiful, wonderful, kind, giving, always there for you, never complaining, always supporting, one who will make you feel like a million dollars even in the worst of times. One who will meet your every need emotionally, physically, and psychologically. One who will give you strong, healthy children—children who are successful and who love and respect you."

Adam asked God, "What is this going to cost me?"

God said, "It will cost you an arm and a leg."

With that, Adam thought for a while and said, "What can I get with a rib?"

In spite of how we feel about relationships, God created us, designed us, and wishes us to be contributing members of his family. God wants us to be part of the human family and his family.

I have been asked, "Why would God create and allow imperfect people?" I heard Dr. Juan Carlos Ortiz, the pastor of Hispanic ministries of the Crystal Cathedral, answer that question with another question.

He asked rhetorically, "Before your children were born, did you think that you would have perfect children? Knowing that your children would not be perfect, you had children anyway." So God created us. Imperfect? Yes. Why would he create imperfect children? The same reason most people have children. Because he loves them—he loves you and me.

God didn't create a family only to then ask us to retreat into total isolation from our siblings. Don't misunderstand me. The solitary life may be the appropriate way to God for certain people, but it is not for everyone. If it is not for you and you have closed yourself off for decades, like some of those early monks did, it can be a waste of a life. God created us for a purpose. He created us to fulfill his command "Love one another."

To pray without ceasing is to have a mind-set, a paradigm, and an outlook that sees everyone as a child of God, created for a purpose, and as a member of your family. It draws us into active, loving communion with God and with others.

One night when my daughter was four years old, I tucked her into bed and waited to hear her good-night prayers. We got into a conversation and she said, "I hate the bad guys." She thought that this was a good thing to say and believe. What followed was a very interesting theological discussion I'll never forget. There I was with a four-year-old child discussing one of the most profound issues.

"Christina," I queried, "who are the bad people?" She responded that they were the guys who shot everybody and stole everything. As the conversation unfolded, we followed a pattern of logic that led to the conclusion, "The bad people are those who hate."

"So if you hate the bad people, that makes you one of the bad people," I shared with her. "So we must love even the bad people."

She then responded, "Then I'm going to pray for all the bad people that God will turn them into good." My daughter is now a young woman and she still prays the prayer she learned those many years ago, "Dear God, help the bad people to turn good. Amen."

Love is the key to unlock your heart to God's presence. Love starts within us. We need to learn the lessons of Jesus to love the least, the ugly, and the unfortunate. As we learn these lessons, our hearts will become more and more open to God.

If I were asked to look over the past one hundred years and consider the "person of the century," I would have to nominate Mother Teresa. Her heart was open to God and the primary quality of her life was love. She gave everything she had to reach out to the least fortunate on planet earth. She sacrificed everything she had for those who had nothing. Who would disagree that she had a profound connection to God? Her connection came from her love.

Praying without ceasing begins with our opening ourselves to God. This happens through our recognition of God, his faithfulness to his children, and our willingness to love one another. As you learn to pray, you will find the following simple steps helpful.

LEARNING TO PRAY

If prayer is communion with God, then there must be a two-way communication system between us and God. Communion is a oneness. It is like a good marriage. A healthy marriage begins with love and is built and sustained by strong communication. So it is with our relationship with God. First, we need to open our hearts to him in love. Second, we need to take the time to listen when he speaks and this means utilizing good communication skills.

One of the most challenging aspects of communication is balance. Neither person should dump a truckload of words, ideas, or issues on the other. To be understood is both a crucial and difficult part of communication. No one has ever been understood without being heard. It is a question of balance, which often needs to be established in small steps. Therein lies the struggle. Communication between two people requires both listening and understanding. If you wish to communicate with God through prayer, it will take some effort on your part. You need to

- include moments of silence. Give yourself time to listen to the One crying out to us. He is shouting from the mountaintops, but there is so much noise in life that unless you intentionally stop and listen, you cannot hear God's voice;

- meditate on what God says. There are many means and methods for meditation. You can meditate as you stretch your muscles with yoga, or sit in a chapel and gaze upon the art, or go to the mountains or the sea and feel the winds of nature;

- add Scripture to your meditation because it creates communion.

Some practical suggestions include these:

- Take a positive verse from the Bible and memorize it. It doesn't have to be word for word; you simply need the gist of the message from the text. If this is uncomfortable for you, you can start with some short, easy verses like "God is Love," "With God all things are possible," or "Ask and it shall be given to you."

- While you meditate in church, at home, in the mountains, or by the sea, keep these words in your thoughts and seek God's guidance for you through them.

I discovered the above method of meditation through my preaching. I was ordained a minister in the Reformed Church in America on September 21, 1980. Part of my training for ministry was sermon preparation. Using a church calendar, I was taught to plan out my sermons months ahead of time. My goal in preaching class was to have the texts and corresponding sermon titles laid out for an entire year. I passed my preaching classes with flying colors and have been following the method I learned there ever since. For over twenty years I have been delivering messages based upon a text from the Bible.

The week before I deliver a message to the congregation, I begin meditating on the chosen passage. Throughout the week, I reflect upon this passage and allow the Holy Spirit to speak to me through those words. This has been the single most powerful way God has spoken to me.

You don't have to be an ordained pastor or leader of a Bible study class to use this. You can simply focus on any passage of Scripture you choose to help you through the day or week.

Choose the text that is right for you. One method is to let the Bible fall open, close your eyes, place your finger on the page, and see what you get. I know many people who use this method, and I have heard some impressive stories about how God revealed to them exactly the sort of message they needed. Although this can work successfully from time to time, I would suggest a more systematic approach on a regular basis.

One such approach is to read through the Bible until you hit upon something that jumps out at you. It can be a verse or idea that you know you need to reflect on.

Another approach that may work even better is making use of a daily devotional. Read the devotion that is chosen to fit with the day and season and reflect upon the words of the author and the text. This will give you a wealth of material to meditate on while you take your quiet time on the beach, in your car, or wherever you decide to listen to God.

As you meditate upon these truths, God will speak to you in ideas, thoughts, or visions. Sometimes it is not altogether clear whether the voice we hear within us is from God or just our own imagination. If there is any question which is which, you need to seek counsel from a friend, mentor, pastor, parent, or all of the above. (Warning: Do not go to people and say, "God told me . . ." Instead, use the words "I think God wants me to . . .")

God's will for your life will become very clear. The next step in choosing to pray without ceasing is to follow through with the thoughts and ideas that God has given you.

FOLLOW GOD'S PLAN

The story is told of a man who lived an ordinary life. He never followed his dreams. He never pursued his desires. Out of a fear of failure he always played it safe. He was a great employee because he never rocked the boat. He would do anything to keep his job. He wasn't late for work, was rarely absent, and always did what was required. When push came to shove, his work came first.

Day after day, year after year, he clocked in and clocked out, collected his paycheck, and hated every minute of it. He had opportunities to teach, to start his own business, to join charities, and do many other things he would have enjoyed. Sadly, fear kept him from ever doing anything that threatened the security of that paycheck.

Then one day it happened—the single factor that everyone on planet earth has in common, the one common denominator that each person will eventually face. In a flash, he died. He found himself at the gates of heaven. He received the judgment of God, and this was his sentence: "From now on you will see everything you could have done, but never did. You will see all the faces you would have redeemed, but never lifted a finger. You will witness the person you would have been if you had only followed me." He spent eternity seeing the history that never took place, the hopeless lives that would have been saved, and the tragedies that ensued because he chose to live in fear. The Bible promises, "God has not given us a spirit of fear, but of power and of love and of a sound mind" (2 Tim. 1:7).

The good news is that this story isn't true. God won't allow this scenario to take place. He scatters his ideas, dreams, and desires like seed. When they fall on fertile soil, they take root and grow. In other words, his plan has many backups so that his will shall be done. The questions that then remain are these:

- Will you be a part of God's plan?

- Will you participate in the joy of living and fulfilling the desires in your life and having the satisfaction of knowing that your life counted for something, that you made a positive difference?

- Will you choose to follow the path of fear or the path God will reveal to you?

When Jesus called the apostle Peter to follow him, he said, "Peter, follow me and I will make you a fisher of men." Peter was a fisherman on the Lake of Gennesaret. A stranger comes out of nowhere and asks Peter to leave his nets and follow him. Why? He promises Peter that he will catch men, not fish. What might Peter have been thinking when he heard these words?

Jesus hadn't performed any miracles yet. He hadn't preached any sermons and he wasn't teaching in the synagogue. All Jesus said was "Follow me" and Peter accepted and obeyed that call. How many times had Jesus said those words, only to receive rejection? The Bible doesn't tell us everything. Peter was the first who didn't reject the offer. The bottom line is that Peter followed Jesus and changed history.

That same invitation comes to each of us. We must ask ourselves, "Will I follow him?" or "Will I succumb to my fears?"

Possibility Living embraces the call and follows Jesus wherever he leads.

LIVE IT UP!

Earlier we talked about A.D.I.O. *(Above, Down, Inside, Out)*. In prayer and meditation, we turn it around to O.I.U.A. We are affected by what happens to us in our lives and in our environment: outside events have their impact on us on the inside, on our hearts and souls. And when our heart becomes troubled or confused, the only direction to go for help is *up*, up to God above.

Things happen. Unexpected tragedies take place in millions of lives every day. Like a boxer in a fight, we take a right hook from the outside and then an unexpected left hook flies in through our defenses with enough power to knock our lights out. Something you thought could never happen to you suddenly decks you, like . . .

"I thought marriage was for a lifetime."

"You're laying me off?"

"I have cancer?"

"He died? He was only eleven."

"The fire took everything."

You probably could add one of your own. If you are alive, there will come a time when you will have to "live it up." The pain and stress will be so great that there is no way for you to do it on your own. That is when A.D.I.O. turns into O.I.U.A. *Outside* events have impinged on what's inside of you, causing suffering and emotional turmoil. You need help, and the only way to turn is *up*, up to God *above*, who alone can hear and answer your prayers.

As servants of God we normally live A.D.I.O. The healthy lifestyle is A.D.I.O. We pray without ceasing, with a "God mind-set." We allow his Spirit to empower us with his presence and we use our newfound joy, peace, love, confidence, and assurance to help others and make this world just a little better.

But when we are hurt it is time to turn it all around and pray as Paul suggests:

> And the Holy Spirit helps us in our distress. For we don't even know what we should pray for, nor how we should pray. But the Holy Spirit prays for us with groaning that cannot be expressed in words. And the Father who knows all hearts knows what the Spirit is saying, for the Spirit pleads for us believers in harmony with God's own will.
>
> Romans 8:26–28

ACCEPTING GOD'S HELP

One of the more difficult things for positive, healthy people to do is to accept help and gifts from others. They are producers, not consumers, and they know it. They pay their taxes and give to their churches. They never steal, cheat, or accept something for nothing. They are the backbone of this nation. When tragedy comes in life, it is very difficult for them to be on the receiving end. This is true even when the help comes from God.

I know what it's like to be on the receiving end. In 1983, I went through the most difficult time of my life. As I mentioned earlier, I was ordained in the Crystal Cathedral in 1980. Two years later, I was pastoring a church in San Juan Capistrano. We had been given that ninety-seven-acre parcel of land, and after much pain and struggle we finally moved into and dedicated our first church building on the Ranch at San Juan Capistrano.

Even though things were going well in the church, things were not going well at home. My wife and I were married in 1974. I was nineteen and she was eighteen. We were too young and immature for marriage, but we believed that we would be happy together forever. We weren't married for more than a few months when she came to me for the first time and said, "I want a divorce." I reminded her that we had many options, but that wasn't one of them. We had made a commitment to each other and to God in front of nearly a thousand witnesses. We had vowed, "For better or worse, richer or poorer, in sickness and health, till death do us part." That meant that we had to make it work. We went to counseling and prayed a lot. The one thing we had in common was we were both dedicated Christians.

Nine years and two children later she said it again. We went to yet another counselor. This time she asked us, "Do you want this marriage to work?" She started with me and I gave the required answer. After all, I believed there was no other option. Then she turned to my wife, who didn't follow the script. She said no. That one word cut deeper than any knife or sword could have. It cut to the marrow of my being. What would happen with my children? Was I worthy to be in ministry if I couldn't keep my family together?

In an attempt to save the marriage, the counselor asked my wife to stay in the relationship for another three months through the holidays. As Christmas approached, the pain became greater and greater. I would tuck Angie and Bobby in bed and wonder, "How could I live without the freedom to kiss them good night every evening?" The pain was particularly intense because I didn't share it with anyone. I believed that if I told anyone, it would hurt my chances of reconciliation. I kept all my feelings inside, knowing that every day the inevitable came a little closer.

Finally, on December 26, 1983, I could take no more. My emotions were out of control. I saw my children playing with their Christmas toys and started crying. I excused myself and retreated into the bathroom to wail. Tears rolled down my face as I held my head with my hands. The pain was so great that my neck could not physically hold up my head. After what seemed like an eternity, I composed myself and tried to go play with the children. A few moments later, the same thing started all over again. After a morning of this, I couldn't take any more, and I packed up a small bag and left.

The pain didn't end there. It wasn't long until the papers were served. All the questions I asked myself from the beginning remained. I didn't know how I could continue with my work as a pastor. There were scriptures in the Bible that caused me concern. I wrote a book during this time entitled *Getting Through the Going Through Stage*, based on Psalm 23. And the title comes from the verse, "Yea, though I go through the valley of the shadow of death, I will fear no evil." God doesn't dump us in the valley. He leads us through. It may feel like you are in a grave, but it is a valley and you can find a way out. "God always provides a way of escape, that you may be able to bear it" (1 Cor. 10:13).

The first scripture that caused me concern said, "A bishop [or a minister] must be blameless, a husband of one wife . . . and one who rules his own house well. . . . For if a man does not know how to rule his own house, how will he take care of the Church of God?" (1 Tim. 3:2–5). I thought my ministry was over and felt that my schooling had been wasted—my usefulness as a minister was behind me.

The second scripture that bothered me was Jesus' words, "And I say to you, whoever divorces his wife except for sexual immorality and marries another commits adultery. And whoever marries her who is divorced commits adultery" (Matt. 5:32). This one led me to believe that since I was divorced, I should live a celibate life and never remarry.

I reasoned that if I could not resolve these scriptures in my mind, I could no longer be a minister. But the promises of God are so true and so real. He says, "All things work together for good to those who love Him, who are called according to His purpose" (Rom. 8:28). I continued to study these scriptures.

The first scripture wasn't very difficult. In the time of Christ, polygamy was common. This passage is not against divorce, but against polygamy and chaos. As a bishop or minister I could not be married to more than one woman at a time and must be in reasonable control of my household. This last clause is really up for interpretation. Everyone needs to know that in my current marriage I rule the roost, but my wife rules the rooster. All kidding aside, to "rule his own house" does not mean to be a big boss at home controlling all the affairs of the family and having the perfect kids. If that were the case, we would have no ministers or bishops. I won't go into what kind of "preacher's kid" I was, but know that there are some interesting stories floating around out there by my Sunday school teachers. The phrase "rule his own house" simply means we need to be able to manage our personal affairs. Someone without the ability to manage his or her own life, probably does not have the requisite administrative ability to lead a church.

The case against remarriage was a little more difficult. Studying the passage on divorce one morning, I looked through my library and discovered a wonderful commentary. This commentary actually came from the writings of a very conservative theologian named C. H. Lenske. My great-uncle Henry had left me his library when he passed away at the age of ninety-three. He is the one who had called my father into the ministry when he told him at the age of five, "Bob, you should be a minister when you grow up."

Troubled by the idea of never being able to pastor a church or marry again, I began to read Lenske's commentaries. While reading, I discovered that there is no passive verb in Greek for the word "to commit adultery." In the Greek mind committing adultery required active participation; it was not something that could be done to one person by another without the first person's involvement.

Yet the text sought to express a passive without having the form to do so. Lenske says in attempting to "bring out the passive sense of the Greek forms," we "translate the words as an infinitive": "causes her *to commit* adultery." In doing so the English acquires and active sense it was never meant to have. He suggests "she is stigmatized as an adulteress" as a better translation. Nothing in the words of Jesus forbids such a woman, or in the reverse case such a man, to marry again. Lenske went on to write, "Such a prohibition is always presumed, but without the least warrant in Jesus' own words. It is this false presumption that causes the current mistranslation."[1]

Today, I can tell you that I have been happily married for many years, and I have two more beautiful children. My oldest children lived with me for the first five years after the divorce. So I was able to hear their nighttime prayers often. They have both grown into well-adjusted, mature young adults and are both committed to Jesus Christ. I am very proud of them.

CONCLUSION

I would never have made it without my faith in God and prayer. It is no wonder that people commit suicide. Without having discovered that there is a way out and that God is in control, I would have been hopeless and desperate.

Knowing that God is there and that I can take my concerns up to him brought me through the valley of the shadow of death. Remember: when you think there is no way out and you feel you are in a grave instead of a valley, look up. The Son will shine down on you and give you the light of hope. Live it up.

Prayer works. Choose prayer. Open up to him. Hear his voice. Follow his plan and live it up.

CHAPTER 8

CHOOSE FASTING

Dr. Douglas Di Siena

As you begin reading, you are probably having thoughts of food. Food controls a good part of our existence. We eat for many reasons:

- because the clock says it is time to eat, even though we may not be hungry

- for comfort or to escape negative feelings

- when we are bored

- as a result of social obligation

As a teenager, I constantly grazed on anything I could find in the refrigerator. The habit of eating when we are not hungry is one reason for our overweight society. Fasting is a wonderful opportunity for us to develop discipline in our lives.

Most people do not wake up and think, "What kind of fast will I start today?" After all, some of us spend a good portion of our day thinking about food, preparing food, or eating food. I know in my Italian family, food is a celebration of daily life. During breakfast, we think about what we will have for lunch. And over lunch—yes, you guessed it, we talk about what's for dinner. Mealtime is an important time for family and friends. Nonetheless, God created us so we eat to live; we do not live to eat.

Many religions, including Judaism and some Christian traditions, use fasting not only as a physical cleansing, but as emotional and spiritual cleansing as well. There are times in your life when it is important to choose fasting in order to experience God's input from above.

The first time fasting was mentioned to me, I tuned out. I wanted no part of anything that would keep me from food and all the pleasure it brought me. I had zero desire to learn about the benefits of fasting. As a doctor, I knew how beneficial fasting is for both the body and soul, yet because food meant so much to me, I did not fast for years. Finally, at my wife's urging we fasted together, and in so doing I discovered another dimension of Possibility Living. Now we routinely go on five-day juice fasts. The benefits for the body, mind, and spirit are extraordinary.

UNDERSTANDING FASTING

Fasting has its own dynamic:

> Day 1 of a fast, you get hungry, the stomach growls, and food has an increased aroma that further temps you to break the fast.

> Day 2 ushers in a sense of deprivation and irritability.

> Day 3 turns the corner and eating loses its appeal.

The initial feeling of hunger is replaced by a heightened sensitivity to the body, the environment, and God's presence. This in turn allows you to think more clearly, have more energy, and lose most, if not all, craving for food. At this point in a fast, you will begin to notice an incredible feeling of accomplishment and spiritual awareness.

So what's fasting? So many people use the term, yet it means different things to different people. I have found that even within the health-care professions, we end up talking about dissimilar things when we use the term "fasting." Fasting is defined as the total abstinence from all food or drink for a definite period of time. The verb "to fast" comes from the English word "to fasten," "to make firm or fixed." Fasting is a very controlled action with a specific goal—to cleanse, heal, or facilitate spiritually reconnection.

Although fasting means total abstinence, we will discuss it not only as absolute abstinence from all food and drink, but also as a restrictive diet. Technically, a juice fast is an oxymoron. A person couldn't be fasting and consuming a juice at the same time. However, for our purposes, a juice fast means restricting the diet to juices, a water fast, to only water, and so on.

The father of medicine, Hippocrates, commented on fasting this way: "Everyone has a doctor in him or her; we just have to help it in its work. The natural healing force within each one of us is the greatest force in getting well. Our food should be our medicine. Our medicine should be our food. But to eat when you are sick is to feed your sickness."

An absolute fast is never recommended and can be quite dangerous physically. The water fast involves a short-term avoidance of all food and other beverages with the exception of vitamins, minerals, and enzymes. I would not recommend a water fast for your first fasting experience. However, a water fast is the best overall cleanser of the body. It requires both strict discipline and complete rest—no work, intense exercise, or stress of any kind—but leads most people into a good space for both prayer and meditation.

One concern with a water fast is the potential for a rapid change in your mineral balance (electrolytes), as well as the possibility for rapid weight loss. The potential rebound effect is a rapid gain of weight after the fasting has stopped. Good health is essential for a water fast to be a safe process.

A partial fast is the most popular type today. The key element here is to eliminate some or most foods in your normal diet. This type of fast is also very useful for cleansing and detoxification purposes. Partial fasts are easier, because when you subsist on a limited diet your blood-sugar level never drops too low. The advantage here, other than that a partial fast is easier to tolerate, is that as you go off the fast, there is less chance that you will gain back the weight.

THE BENEFITS OF FASTING

Fasting encourages the body to go into healing mode. Fasting follows the law of the conservation of energy. The body has a limited amount of energy to carry on the tasks necessary to keep us alive and functioning in our environment. Fasting is a way to give our body the rest it needs from the day-to-day rigors required for the digestion and elimination processes and to free up that energy for healing purposes.

Consider for a moment how miraculous the body is. For instance, think about what you had for breakfast. Your body takes that food and then proceeds to expend energy breaking it down into its basic nutritional components. It is amazing to think that each bite we take is broken down into the most elemental components. Carbohydrates are broken down and used for energy. Or if excess is taken in, your body first converts those "carbs" into glycogen to be stored in the muscle or the liver. Fat is broken down by the release of many enzymes including bile. By the way, our bodies need fat for hormone production, maintaining a healthy nervous system, storing energy, and protecting many of our vital organs. Protein is broken down and used for tissue repair and regeneration. The process of life requires a tremendous amount of energy. During a fast, the energy normally required for the breakdown of food can be used for healing and regeneration.

Fasting concentrates healing energy where it is needed most. The body has a finite reserve of energy. By giving the body and mind a rest during a fast, we will have increased energy and vitality for healing.

Fasting also gives our digestive systems a rest. It gives our detoxing organs a break from any incoming toxins normally accompanying the regular food intake. Organs like the kidney, liver, skin, and colon are then available to remove the toxins stored in the fat layer. Sometime between the second and third day of the fast, the body must dip into the fat cells for energy. As the body begins to break down this stored fat, it is able to give full attention to metabolizing out of the body all of the stored toxins. Be aware that mild symptoms from released toxins could return. Although this may be unpleasant for a short time, the good news is the body finally has a chance to deal with these stored toxins and expel them from the system. This is one of the many reasons why a person should always be closely supervised by a doctor or qualified health-care provider during a fast.

Felix L. Oswald, M.D., explains it well:

> With no digestive drudgery on hand, nature employs the long-desired leisure for general house-cleaning purposes. The accumulations of superfluous tissues are overhauled and analyzed; the available component parts are turned over to the department of nutrition, the refuse to be thoroughly and permanently removed.[1]

Let us review a few of the many benefits that fasting offers the body, mind, and spirit:

- discipline
- heightened spiritual awareness, and an intimacy with God and his will for your life
- spiritual healing
- emotional cleansing
- restoration of biochemical balance
- increased oxygenation throughout the body
- increased ability for the mobilization of white blood cells
- increased awareness of the body for the purpose of detecting toxic tissue
- enhanced ability for the body to detoxify
- weight loss
- stimulation of the immune function through the elimination of toxins in the body and a decrease in the food-borne allergic response

Now that we have emphasized some of the benefits of fasting, we must give a warning. Let us emphatically say here that all forms of fasting have a small potential for ill effects. Fasting should only be done with the advice and supervision of an experienced, qualified health-care professional.

Some of those who might have problems fasting are these:

- people in any type of crisis/critical care or who are otherwise very unhealthy

- people just recovering from acute or crisis care

- people who are underweight

- people with any acute respiratory dysfunction

- people with eating disorders

- people with unstable sugar levels

- women who are pregnant

If you are on any medications, please see the prescribing doctor to make sure they would cause no adverse effects during a fast.

Many believe that fasting cleanses the body, but assume that it leaves us tired, sick, and hungry. The reality is, in fact, the exact opposite. Fasting provides us with the following:

1. *Increased energy.* The first paradox is that, although you think fasting will cause you to lose strength and endurance, once the body begins to understand that food will not be around for a while, your energy levels actually rise.

2. *Increased healing.* Although it may seem that food is necessary for healing, fasting helps release energy already stored in the body. With the proper type of fast, this energy is freed up for healing. Most important, by fasting for a time we avoid many of the toxins that the body normally has to deal with.

3. *Fewer food cravings.* The most unusual paradox is the diminishment of food cravings. Sometimes I become concerned when people go on extended fasts, because it is easy to lose the sensation of hunger. I was talking to a patient of mine who regularly goes on fasts. She said the most difficult part for her is not going on the fast, but coming off it. The body feels so clean and pure that you do not want to pollute it.

4. *Increased aptitude for taste.* This is one of the strangest benefits of fasting. One might think that fasting would cause you to lose your sensory aptitude for taste. Yet the opposite is true. After fasting, every bite of every food you eat is enjoyed with new appreciation. There is no longer the need to put excessive fat, salt, or sugar in food for taste. In fact, extra fat and sugar become very unsettling to the stomach. The effect is similar to the one resulting from the change in American milk-drinking habits. Today most people drink lowfat or nonfat rather than whole milk, and many who grew up on whole milk can no longer tolerate the "richness" of it.

HOW TO FAST

Every fast has basic elements to keep in mind. Let us walk you through these steps.

Preparation

Before beginning a fast, the soul must be free of fear, apprehension, and anxiety. If you are considering a fast, you must be completely honest with your health-care professional. I know many experts who never let their patients begin a fast with any signs of fear. If you are apprehensive in any way, we recommend starting on a restrictive diet. Also, much reassuring information about fasting can be found in *Fasting Can Save Your Life,* by Herbert M. Shelton, and *The Roots and Fruits of Fasting,* by Dr. Mary Swope.[2]

My good friend Dr. Shalhoub often says, "Knowledge is not power, truth is power." I believe if we just took the time to learn the truth, especially when it relates to our own health and well-being, we would become empowered to make the right choices, giving us the best opportunity for a life of wellness. Thus part of the preparation should be to become a student of fasting. Everything about the spiritual, emotional, and physical aspects of fasting can be studied. Understanding the process of fasting will ease most of the anxiety that accompanies the first fast. As you prepare, tell those close to you what you are about to do. You certainly will need support, especially the first day, which in my experience is the most difficult day.

Relax: A Fast Should Be Calming, Not Anxiety-Producing

A fast should not make you sick. Fasting is not about going around feeling, acting, or looking miserable. You may have a few temporary, unpleasant feelings at the beginning, but if you do notice any continuing ill effects, stop the fast and seek the advice of your health-care professional. Especially after the first day, fasting will make you feel better.

Fasting Should Be Refreshing, Cleansing, and Renewing

Jesus never commanded us to fast. He did say that when we fast, we should examine our inner selves and motives. Do not fast to impress others. Jesus said, "When you fast, do not look somber as the hypocrites do, for they disfigure their faces to show men they are fasting. I tell you the truth, they have received their reward in full" (Matt. 6:16, NIV).

Drink an Abundance of Water

I cannot emphasize enough how important hydration is to the human body when the body is not fasting, let alone when it is. I recommend 64 to 80 ounces of clean, filtered spring water a day for the average-sized person. During a fast, it is better to sip water all day long than to down a 32-ounce bottle a couple of times a day.

Water is a universal solvent and has many unique properties. With the exception of oxygen, there are few things more important to the health and well-being of the body than the regular intake of pure water. I recommend spring or mineral water for its mineral content. Tap water has chlorine and other potentially toxic substances to be avoided, especially during a fast.

Limit Your Activities

On a limited or food-restricted fast, your ability to function at work will not be a problem. However, all forms of exercise should be reduced and mild, as intense or strenuous activity might prove too stressful for the body. As I became accustomed to the juice fast, my daily activities did not need to slow down. But with the stricter water fast, activities should be eliminated or restricted as much as possible.

Rest

Although with a juice fast rest is important, for a water fast rest is essential for the complete cleansing effect to occur. This means both body and soul. Bed rest with little sensory stimuli is highly recommended. This is the perfect time for spiritual meditation, contemplation, and reflection. As we said above, avoidance of physical and mental stimulation helps allow the body to put its full energy into the clearing of the toxins, healing of the tissues, and the regeneration of healthy tissue.

Exposure to Natural Sunlight

Seek exposure to sunlight for up to fifteen to thirty minutes a day, preferably in the morning or late afternoon when the rays are less intense. Sunlight can have a very calming action on the soul. Sunlight helps with vitamin D formation, which is critical for preserving bone density. The sun's ultraviolet light naturally kills viruses and bacteria.

Hygiene

Unfortunately, as the body detoxes, there will be some unpleasant body odor. Bathing will help. However, excessive bathing is not recommended, and definitely avoid applying anything to the skin that is laden with chemicals. Additionally, very hot baths can prove to be too stressful for the body. We have found that sitting in a warm, but not hot, bath can ease some of the initial aching that happens in the first day or so of a fast.

Antiperspirants should always be avoided, because of the possibility that the aluminum (usually the active ingredient) can be absorbed through the skin. Most other toiletries that are applied to the skin should be avoided as well, including aftershave, lotion, perfumes, colognes, deodorants, foot sprays, and so on. Tooth brushing should be done as usual, but with a natural toothpaste. I would also recommend brushing the back of the tongue, which helps remove impurities. Dentures should be left in and worn normally during the fast. If left out, the gums might experience some shrinkage. See your dentist for any questions related to dentures.

Completing the Fast

Coming off of the fast is in many ways more critical than preparing for it. I know many people who set a goal for a five-day fast. Everything is going well until the fourth day when, suddenly, the body begins to feel strong hunger pangs. That is the body signaling it is time to end the fast. Remember, during the fast you are hungry only the first day. After that, your hunger actually subsides and you lose the temptation to eat. Whenever those hunger feelings return, or any ill symptoms for that matter, you should begin the process of ending your fast. Your body is telling you that all of the reserves are used up. It is crucial to listen to your body. If you don't give your body food at this point, it will begin the degenerative process of eating away vital protein tissues of organs and muscle.

A fast does not require starvation. To continue the fast after the body signals to eat is to move into starvation. This is not healthy and could be critically dangerous to your health.

If you set out to do a three-day fast, it is not a failure to come off the fast on the second day. Listen and respond appropriately to your body. This is the A.D.I.O. approach. Fasting is about getting connected to God and the temple of the Spirit, your body. In the fast you will become much more aware in general—spiritual, physical, and emotional awareness will all be increased. Listen to God's still small voice (1 Kings 19:12, KJV).

Coming off of the fast should take as much time as the actual fast. I use the illustration of an airplane ascending to reach altitude (the preparation), moving along at cruising speed (the actual fast, as much less energy is required), then, as the fuel runs low, gradually descending (coming off of the fast). A gradual decent is necessary to avoid a crash landing. The way to come off the fast is to work into eating very gradually. Do not plan a feast for the end of your fast—that's dangerous.

As you begin the reintroduction of food back into your diet, start with light portions of mild food. Drink juices at first, sipped gradually. Your stomach has probably shrunk and your digestive system needs to slowly get accustomed to working again. If you consume too much food too quickly or it is too spicy, you could be in for some terrible stomachaches and diarrhea as well as other gastrointestinal disturbances.

After a day of juices, introduce light soups, fruits, and my favorite, oatmeal with soy protein, into your diet. At this point, you want to get your protein mostly from the plant kingdom in the form of groundnuts and legumes, especially soy or tofu. I also like chicken broth as a starter food. Depending on the length of the fast, you can then slowly work in larger meals and eventually return to animal protein, if you are so inclined. Coming off of a fast is also a great time to start new healthy dietary habits.

FASTING AND SPIRITUAL GROWTH

As one fasts, the physical benefits soon become pleasantly noticeable. However, connecting to God and spiritual nourishment are probably the greatest gifts fasting has to offer.

Fasting is described in the Scriptures at least thirty times. Although Jesus never suggested or commanded us to fast, we can see in the

Scriptures how people used fasting for an inner cleansing. The biblical sage Daniel fasted with significant spiritual results: "So I gave my attention to the Lord God to seek Him by prayer and supplications, with fasting, sackcloth, and ashes" (Dan. 9:3, NAS).

Fasting is first mentioned in the Scriptures when Moses goes up to Mount Sinai to receive the law. He obviously had a supernatural fast, because the Scriptures say he went without food or water for forty days. "So he was there with the Lord forty days and forty nights; he did not eat bread or drink water. And he wrote on the tablets the words of the covenant, the Ten Commandments" (Exod. 34:28, NAS). Moses later revealed that God commanded his people to take a day for atonement. This custom became known as "the day of fasting" (Jer. 36:6).

At other times in the Bible, whole communities of people fasted for various reasons well outside the law of Moses. They fasted in times of war and as a way for God to protect them on long journeys. They fasted to demonstrate their humility. Israel fasted seven days when Saul and his son were buried.

Like Moses, Jesus started his ministry with a forty-day "supernatural" fast. After being baptized by his cousin John, he was directed by the Holy Spirit to enter into the wilderness and to fast for forty days (Matt. 4:1–2). Both Jesus and Moses had to rely on faith from day to day for God's supernatural sustenance and direction from the Holy Spirit.

Fasting can be used as an exercise for denying the self, thereby allowing us to receive the greatness of God. Jesus instructs us to deny the self: "If anyone would come after me, he must deny himself and take up his cross and follow me" (Mark 8:34, NIV).

Through fasting we discipline ourselves to overcome trivial thoughts, habits, and desires and to become more like Jesus. In many ways, we are constantly tempted and tried as we grow spiritually. I know people who come to know God and develop a personal relationship with him only to face crisis, trial, and temptation in life. But through trials we develop a deeper faith. Paul writes, "Not only so, but we also rejoice in our sufferings, because we know that suffering produces perseverance; perseverance, character; and character, hope. And hope does not disappoint us, because God has poured out his love into our hearts by the Holy Spirit, whom he has given us" (Rom. 5:3–5, NIV).

Through trials, we develop a deeper reliance upon God. In all our crises, we can rely on the promise, "And the peace of God, which transcends all understanding, will guard your hearts and your minds in Christ Jesus" (Phil. 4:7, NIV).

Many people attempt to attain a sense of peace in the short term such as going on an exotic vacation. For instance, how hard is it to feel at peace lying on a warm beach under a palm tree on a secluded tropical island? That doesn't take any faith or reliance on God. True long term peace can only come from connecting *above down*.

FASTING AND POSSIBILITY LIVING

In Possibility Living, fasting serves the purpose of putting us in a place of returning to God and relying on him for peace, power, and life in all circumstances and every situation. Some spiritual benefits of fasting include these:

- *Fasting gives us clarification.* The Scriptures offer us an example of St. Paul and Barnabas praying and fasting before making the decision for a God-inspired appointment of the elders of the church. "Paul and Barnabas prayed with fasting at the appointment of elders in the churches" (Acts 14:23).

- *Fasting helps us sort through our decisions with God's guidance.* Fasting puts us in a place with God so that we can clearly sort through our decisions with his help. When you choose to fast, make that moment a defining moment in which you commit your body as living sacrifice to God (Rom. 12:1–2).

- *Fasting gives us an opportunity to change bad habits and negative attitudes.* During and following a fast, you will discover the Spirit's power to help change bad habits and negative attitudes. Your body is cleansed and refreshed, your appetite is more in tune with the body's needs, and you are absorbing more vitamins and minerals from the food you eat. During a fast, pray through any problems you face and the changes you would like to make, and seek God's guidance in how to implement them positively.

After you fast, reaffirm your commitment to the temple of God, your body, of which you must be a good steward. Take care of your body, and your body will take care of you. It is the only body you will have this side of heaven. Treat it well—it's your physical vehicle for moving through life filled with God's awesome possibilities.

CHAPTER 9

DETOXIFY YOUR RELATIONSHIPS

Dr. Robert A. Schuller

We have been sharing with you how to make right choices as you pursue Possibility Living. Let us now turn our attention to detoxifying our lives. Toxins are negative, destructive, and hurtful agents in life that rob you of life's possibilities on any level—physical, emotional, or spiritual. One of the most destructive agents for your soul is a toxic relationship. Possibility Living transforms toxic relationships into nourishing ones. We also learn in Possibility Living how to honor and love everyone, including our enemies, while purging and cleansing ourselves of the toxic relationships that harm and hurt us.

I have a good friend who has not seen her parents for several years. They live less than two miles away, yet she will not talk to them. She doesn't know if she will ever be able to see them again. She was once the apple of her father's eye. However, the immense amount of emotional baggage connected with all of her family's interpersonal issues is just too much for her to bear. Her family relationships are so toxic that she is afraid to reenter her family circle. She shared with me, "My health and the health of my family emotionally, physically, and spiritually will not allow me to be with them." Although she loves and honors her family, she has purged herself of negative contact with them and the negative attitudes toward them she used to carry.

There are times when a relationship is so toxic that removing oneself from it is the only recourse. Apart from those extreme cases, most toxic relationships can be turned into tolerable, if not positive, ones.

WHAT ARE TOXIC RELATIONSHIPS?

Certain people always bring out the worst in us. For some reason when they are around, our personality defects are magnified and intensified. For example, if I have a smoking habit (and I don't) and am trying to quit, a toxic relationship can drive me right back to smoking. As a result, I may have to avoid that relationship in an attempt to maintain my emotional and even physical health.

As a parent, I am concerned about protecting my children from toxic relationships as they grow up. There are certain children I do not want my son or daughter to have as friends because they make poor choices in their words or actions.

I recently read the story of Cassie Bernall shortly after I interviewed her parents on the "Hour of Power" telecast. You may remember that she was the seventeen-year-old girl who was shot and killed at Columbine High in Littleton, Colorado. *She Said Yes* is the title of the book her mother, Misty, wrote about her. The book's title tells her story. When the shooters came to Cassie and asked her if she believed in God, she said yes. In her book, Cassie's mother shares the incredible transformation that took place in Cassie's life before that tragic day at Columbine.

Cassie had many toxic relationships. Her friends pulled her into all kinds of dark and oppressive behavior. Even though Misty had suspicions of what her daughter was doing, she really couldn't even imagine how deep her daughter's negativity had become. It came to a head when Misty was cleaning out Cassie's room and found some letters from her friends and letters she had written but never mailed. In the correspondence, there were plans to kill her mother, father, and teachers. She had become involved with such an evil group that her parents had little choice but to cut her off from all association with those young people. They put her in a private Christian school, but that wasn't enough. The kids kept hanging around the neighborhood and other places where they might see Cassie. Finally, the family felt that the only recourse was to move.

It was at a summer camp in the mountains where Cassie's life changed. She was released from her torment of hatred and found a new life—a life of love. She didn't become an overnight saint; she still had a lot of spiritual growing to do. But by the end of summer her life and outlook had changed and her parents felt that it was safe for her to return to public school. She enrolled at Columbine. On April 20, 1999, she said yes and her brush with death was turned into eternal life.

If you read the book, you will see the potential dangers of toxic relationships. Few associations can be as toxic as Cassie's were, but the fact remains that, throughout our lives, peer pressure continues to be a powerful influence. As a rule, we often resemble those people with whom we spend a lot of time.

I have traveled all over the world and one of the clichés I follow is, "When in Rome, do as the Romans do." It simply means, follow the customs of the culture you are in. If you are in Morocco, you eat with your hands. If you are in Hawaii, you wear shorts. It is not only a natural thing to want to fit in, but that is the way God wired us when he created us. This natural instinct works well when we are in positive and healthy relationships and situations. Unfortunately, in negative relationships, we cannot do as others do, because their destructive thoughts and behaviors will hurt us. Until we have well-established boundaries and a clear understanding of who we are, we will think like and become like those we associate with.

As a parent, I see this very clearly. We know that if our children choose the wrong friends and start hanging with the wrong crowd, it will lead to trouble. As adults, we seem to think we are immune to association. We are not. Positive and healthy relationships can yield endless benefits; negative and toxic associations can spell serious danger.

From a spiritual perspective, one of the main reasons we need to attend church is to be able to associate with positive and loving people. We learn not only about the Bible, but also receive the benefits of associating with people who share our spiritual interests. This creates a fertile environment for spiritual growth.

HANDLING TOXIC PEOPLE WE MUST FACE

Some relationships are almost impossible to avoid. We did not choose our parents, children, or siblings. We are in our families because God wanted us there. He gave them to us and we need to make our relationships positive. But how? Many problems with conflict in relationships arise out of our families. Clearly much of the professional counseling done by psychologists focuses on family members—husbands and wives, parents and children. When relationships in the family turn toxic, it is important to work through the negatives and turn them into positives.

Besides the family, there may be other toxic relationships you must face—people at work, in school, or in the neighborhood who can be difficult to relate to. They may be rude, insulting, stubborn, belittling, demeaning, and so on. No matter where you go, there will always be some of these types around. You cannot avoid them.

Avoiding all "toxic people" is impossible. They cut you off on the freeway. They criticize you to the boss. They make unreasonable demands and gossip behind your back. Nothing you do or say seems to affect the toxicity they pour into your life. No matter what you do, there will always be toxic people in your life. The good news is that you can take positive actions to detoxify and protect yourself from their effect.

Let's begin by first discussing how we detoxify negative family situations, then move into business and work issues, and finally discuss how to handle the stranger who tries to poison your day. Possibility Living can dilute the effects of all such toxic people with the antidote of love.

COPING WITH TOXIC FAMILY RELATIONSHIPS

Having been raised in an intact nuclear family, I grew up with both parents at home. Dad went to work every morning, and Mom was a homemaker. I have four sisters—one is older and three are younger.

The challenge for us was being in the spotlight. We lived in the fishbowl of a church and ministry in which my father was a well-known pastor and television personality.

I now have a family of my own with four children—two in college and two in middle school. The oldest are from my first marriage. When my sisters and I and our families gather at our parents' home, it's quite an event. Five children are on the scene—all married, with eighteen grandchildren. That's a grand total of thirty. We all—children, spouses, parents—are employed in the Crystal Cathedral Ministries.

I share this with you to let you know that, as in most families, peculiar dynamics go on when we all get together. I have had to learn to practice the communications skills I preach. No one is immune to the toxic effects that can arise from family relationships. Throughout the years, we have gone through tragedy and ecstasy; we have cried and laughed, disagreed and argued, grieved and rejoiced.

Dr. Kevin Leman, in his book *The Birth Order*, tells how the birth order in a family has a dramatic impact on our personalities. Much of who we are and how we perceive things is determined by our birth order. The firstborn child is the prince or princess. He or she cuts the path for the second-born, who will be the baby if he or she is the last child. He goes on to explain all the different scenarios that take place with each additional child and how they work. Since *Possibility Living* is not designed to take you through all the mechanics of relationships, I would suggest reading this book if you are interested in the inner workings of your family and your role is in it.

We want to foster nurturing and healthy relationships in your family and help you to create positive support systems. The steps in this process begin with self-reflection, continue with conflict resolution, and conclude with how to maintain healthy boundaries.

POSSIBILITY LIVING CHOOSES HEALTHY RELATIONSHIPS

Step 1: Self-reflection

I have a hobby that began when I was very young. I love to fish. Some of my earliest memories of fishing include going to the Newport Pier with my father. I also went fishing with my uncle. He would take me to the back of his farm to fish the Floyd River in northwest Iowa. This was where my father fished for the first time. It is not a world-class fishing destination, but it does have bullheads up to five inches long and an occasional carp.

Today, I participate in world-class marlin tournaments. (I have done quite well. In fact, my accountant says that I have won enough money and prizes to be considered a professional, but this only means that I can write off some of the expenses associated with my hobby.) In order to fish, we must often go several miles off shore. As we travel out in the ocean, we look for signs of life. When we reach the right area, we can see the top layer of the food chain. It begins with plankton, extends to bait fish, and finally concludes with the game fish we want. This island of life swims around, and we follow it looking for the marlin that feed in it.

At the end of the day, the first thing we must do is calculate our location. We must know where we are before we can determine our course to the marina. It is very humbling being in the middle of the ocean. Everywhere you look there's nothing but water—it looks the same in every direction.

Just as it is imperative for fishermen to know their position in order to find their way home, it is crucial for us to find and understand ourselves so that we can enjoy the rewards of healthy, positive, nourishing relationships. This begins by learning as much about ourselves as possible. Just as there are tools to help sailors and fisherman find their position in the ocean, we have tools to help us understand where we are as individuals and how to relate to those around us.

The most important tool for understanding ourselves and our relationships is the Bible. In Scripture, we discover that God has given each of us a unique personality for relating to others as well as the power to change and grow.

You have a unique, God-given personality. In our Possibility Living seminars at Rancho Capistrano, we offer a personality survey. There are several different surveys available. The one I like most is taken from the book *Please Understand Me* by David Keirsy and Marilyn Bates.

This book is a solid resource and gives all the basic personality information necessary for an accurate reading.

Along with Keirsy and Bates, John Trent and Gary Smalley, authors of *Love is a Decision*, provide a useful approach. By making associations between personality traits and animals, Trent and Smalley demonstrate the ways in which people fall into personality types. For example, some people have characteristics that are similar to those of a lion. Lions are strong leaders who get things done; they are the movers and shakers. Another type is the golden retriever. These people are the lovers, the ones who want to make peace. They are faithful and caring; you can depend on them. Other people resemble otters—playful, happy, and ready for a good time. They are childlike and fun to be around. "Beavers" are the hard workers who are interested in the details. They want the facts right, their ducks in a row, and the "t's" crossed. No single animal type is better than any other, and we all have a little of each animal in us, but one is dominant.

One of the healthiest things that can happen in self-discovery is that we reveal the uniqueness of God's creation. He truly has made all of us with the different gifts. In order to succeed, we need all these unique human qualities working together. Therein lies the beauty of teamwork and family. Each person has many wonderful and special contributions to make in a relationship. Those contributions include the spiritual gifts that God has given us for serving and helping others.

You have spiritual gifts. The second survey we offer at the Possibility Living Seminars is the Spiritual Gifts Survey. This is a tool that enhances our personal knowledge of what God has given us to offer the world. There are many spiritual gifts, far more than the praying, preaching, and teaching that most people think of. The following is a list of spiritual gifts:

administration	knowledge
apostle	leadership
celibacy	martyrdom
discernment	mercy

evangelism	miracles
exhortation	missionary
exorcism	pastor
faith	prophecy
giving	service
healing	teaching
help	tongues
hospitality	voluntary poverty
intercession	wisdom
interpretation	

You may have several gifts. If you read through the list you may be able to say, "Now, I do that." You probably have others that you do not even know about. The survey can be helpful in determining the gifts that you know about, as well as those you have yet to discover.

We have been giving this survey to the new members of our church and they have always been very encouraged with the results. Each person in the church not only cares for others, but also needs to care for themselves. Jesus commanded us to love God, and then to love others as we love ourselves. An important way to care for ourselves is to keep both our bodies and our relationships healthy.

Your body is your temple of the Spirit. Doing what is right for the body will renew your entire person. In order to take steps toward physical success, we need to know where we are. We give blood tests and other physical exams at the Possibility Living Seminars and have helped many people understand how healthy they are and how much work they need to do to obtain optimum wellness.

I became interested in health after I had a standard cholesterol blood test. When it didn't turn out the way I expected, it changed everything. God only knows what condition I would be in today had I not taken that test. Ignorance is bliss, until it kills you. Please take care of yourself. If it has been more than a year since you have seen a health professional, please make an appointment. Also, it is important to see a health-care professional who is concerned about the whole you—body, mind, and spirit.

Step 2: Conflict Resolution

After you have taken the steps to follow the dictum "Know thyself," you are ready to begin dealing with the other half of any toxic relationship—the other person. A main ingredient in all unhealthy relationships is conflict or anger. Conflict resolution and management turn toxic relationships into nourishing ones. And dealing with toxic people requires conflict resolution. Let us learn more.

Symptoms of conflict may appear in various forms, such as strife, frustration, anger, or hostility, yet they arise from the same root. Whatever type you are experiencing—a personality conflict, a conflict of wills, or one of spirit—resolution is the key. Resolving the conflict will produce great benefits to your health—physically, emotionally, and spiritually.

My father told me years ago that "conflict is a result of unmet expectations." In general, I agree with that statement, and in this section we will discuss this kind of conflict. However, there are other situations in which it is not a matter of unmet expectations, but greedy aggression. Sometimes people are motivated by nothing more than their own personal agendas and are willing to do whatever is necessary to accomplish their goals even if it means hurting others in the process. Conflict in these situations may be impossible to resolve, and then we must rely on management and maintaining healthy boundaries, which we will cover in Step 3.

Unmet expectations occur often. I don't believe there has been a marriage in the history of humankind that did not have this problem. Think about the expectations the groom has about his wife-to-be and the bride has about her husband-to-be. Most of our expectations are subconscious. They have been taught culturally or modeled by our parents.

The first day after the honeymoon Harry roles out of bed, hops in the shower, and leaves for work early without saying a word. He wants to let Mary sleep in. That is what his father always did, and now that he is married that is what he is supposed to do. Mary wakes up a few minutes after Harry has gone. Where is he? Maybe he went to the grocery store to buy something for breakfast? After all her father always made breakfast before he left for work. Where is breakfast? As she waits, she realizes that not only is he not bringing breakfast, but he isn't coming back until the end of the day. On top of that, he didn't even say good-bye! To make matters worse, Mary hasn't figured out that Harry, like his father, expects dinner to be waiting for him when he comes home.

I don't think I need to go on. Harry and Mary have some unmet expectations that have caused conflict. You can see how conflict between two very loving people can erupt. It can happen over something as simple as making the bed. I once counseled a woman who was having problems in her marriage because of toilet paper! Granted toilet paper is important, but if you cannot resolve a toilet paper conflict, you really need to read this section several times over. Let me suggest the following:

Expect Conflict. The more you associate with someone, the more conflict you will experience. If you expect it, it won't be a surprise. The expected isn't as frightening. If you fear something, you naturally become defensive. In relationships, our defenses often take the form of walls, and the way we learned to defend ourselves during childhood determines what kind of walls we build. Relational walls can look like the following:

- *Stone walls* result in emotional shut-down. This is a response to the most dangerous and toxic form of conflict. If it continues for an extended period of time, it can become clinical depression. Depression is often confused with grief, sorrow, or sadness. Depression is not bad feelings, but *no* feelings. Depression takes place when we are emotionally flat-lined. If you are in a hospital and you flat-line on the monitor, the bells and whistles sound and the doctors and nurses do everything possible to revive you. Thousands of people have flat-lined emotionally, but there are no bells and whistles sounding and no doctors and nurses running to their aid. They have chosen to defend themselves by turning them off. They have died emotionally. If you fit in this category, you need some help soon. Talk to your pastor or a psychologist as soon as possible.

- *Distance walls* are used for running away. People work extra hours, go shopping, or hit the bottle. Retreat is a common wall of defense against negative, toxic people—they cannot harm you if you run. So off you go into the wild blue yonder, flying high until you crash. Continual overwork results in one thing—burnout. We need to balance our work and play, and we can't do that if we are running. Running initially served a survival purpose; it is one of the primary abilities God gave us to escape physical danger in our environment. But in relationships running goes nowhere; it is usually the defense used when we won't change and grow through the relationship. We need to stand up to the toxic people and make them our allies, not our foes.

- *Offensive walls* offer a good offense as the best defense. People using offensive walls become aggressive. Scary people often have a strong exterior—a lion personality—with a weak interior. They will run right over you if you are not careful and push you around. They wear their feelings on their sleeves and are usually unreasonable. You always know where they stand, there are no hidden agendas, and they tell it like they see it. They demand respect and usually get it.

- *Self-denial walls* are used by people who refuse to make waves. People in self-denial believe that they cannot get hurt if they please others. They don't do what they want, but try to do whatever keeps peace. Such people brag, "I have never been in an argument with my spouse." Of course not, they simply do whatever the spouse wants. People with low self-esteem often fall into this trap. They don't have enough will to run, enough confidence to stand up for what they believe, or enough strength to be aggressive. Instead of facing the toxic relationship, they deny it exists.

Accept that conflict can be a constructive learning experience. God didn't make us all identical. He made each of us different, with a distinct way of seeing the world. Our individuality gives us multiple ways to solve the same problems. One person isn't necessarily right and the other necessarily wrong. Most conflict isn't right against wrong; it is right against right. It is choosing which path to take in a multipath world. Do we take the north road or the south road? Healthy conflict handled correctly produces a better result.

Through conflict we learn something about each other and our various viewpoints. It usually isn't fun, but it is productive. Accept conflict as part of living and learn to play with it. You don't always have to conclude with an agreement. There are many things loving people will never agree upon. When my wife and I find ourselves in this situation, we agree to disagree.

Seek similarities. Toxic relationships will become healthy as we learn to live in peace. We may not agree on everything, but there are many things we can agree about. My father is a firm believer in the practice of finding common ground. As a result, he has become a peacemaker. Recently, the following news bulletin was released:

CHRISTIAN, MUSLIM LEADERS SEND MESSAGE TO MIDEAST PEACE NEGOTIATORS IN WASHINGTON

Damascus, Dec. 17, 1999: Following today's historic meeting between two of the most influential religious leaders, Reverend Robert H. Schuller and the Syrian Republic's Grand Mufti, the clerics sent a joint message to the Syrian and Israeli peace negotiators in Washington after a phone call was placed to President Clinton.

Their message, from Isaiah 58:12, "You shall become the repairer of the breach, the restorer of paths to dwell in" was quoted earlier in the day by Reverend Schuller, the senior pastor of the Crystal Cathedral Ministries, when he stood beside the Grand Mufti, Sheikh Ahmad Kiftarou, and addressed 15,000 Muslims at the Abou Nour Mosque. It is the first time a Christian leader has been invited by the Grand Mufti to speak at the holy mosque.

After the address, Reverend Schuller said: "We have all failed, Christians and Muslims, to treat each other with respect and dignity, but now that must change." Sheikh Kiftarou added: "I pray that President Clinton will be helped by God in achieving peace in our two countries, between Arabs and Israelis."

The joint appearance of the two religious leaders was called "historic" by Azzaka I, the patriarch of the Syrian Orthodox Church of the World, who told Reverend Schuller: "You are a testament to peace between Muslims and Christians here in Damascus."

Today's meeting comes just 24 hours after Reverend Schuller met with Syrian Vice President Mohammed Zohair Masharqa to discuss the possible peace between Syria and Israel and the role that religion can play in breaching the gap between the two nations.

Tomorrow Reverend Schuller will be in Amman, Jordan, to attend a dinner with King Abdullah of Jordan in honor of his late father, King Hussein, a renowned Mideast peacemaker. On Christmas Eve, Reverend Schuller will hold a candlelight service for 2,000 worshipers in Shepherd's Field, Jerusalem, which will be telecast live via satellite to audiences around the world.

My dad found himself in this position because he has always looked for the similarities. One would think it might be very difficult to see similarities between Christians and Muslims. The fact is, in spite of the centuries of war and bitterness, we have common ground in our religious heritage. If Christians and Muslims can find common ground and work together for peace, I believe that you can find ways to be a peacemaker in the most toxic of relationships. If you focus on the similarities instead of the differences, you will have the necessary attitude to reach a resolution.

Practice responsive listening skills. My wife and I spent a week on Maui in the Hawaiian Islands with David Burns, one of the leading authorities on cognitive therapy. It was a small group of about twenty people. The purpose was to learn better communication skills. We spent a long time practicing and using responsive listening, a priceless tool for dealing with toxic relationships and people.

In responsive listening, we must echo the ideas of the person we are listening to. At first, this will be awkward and cumbersome. I felt silly repeating the same words and thoughts I had just heard my wife say. What I discovered was that often I would repeat the message, only to be told that that was not what she meant. She would go on to clarify her feelings and I would repeat them again. Usually, I got it right the second time, but not always. People want to be heard and understood and this is the best method of letting them know they have been. To be a good responsive listener requires practice, but the results are rewarding.

Give the benefit of the doubt. When in doubt, always give others the benefit. When you doubt the integrity or goodwill of another person's motives, you become distrustful and unwilling to share openly with them. When trust is rebuilt and doubt is removed, the conflict will be nearly over. If you are in doubt about why a person said a certain thing or acted a certain way, choose to believe the best about that person—give him or her the benefit of the doubt. My father has said, "If I'm going to sin, it will be on the side of generosity." Many are so afraid of getting cheated and becoming a target, that they won't give an inch. I would suggest giving a mile and living by faith. Jesus said it this way after St. Peter asked how many times he should forgive his brother, "I tell you, not seven times, but seventy times seven" (Matt. 18:22).

Jesus tells the parable of the ruler who was owed money, but let his debtor off the hook, only to find out that his debtor threw someone else in prison for not paying him a debt. With that, the ruler took retribution (Matt. 18:23–35). The lesson for us is that if God can continually forgive us, why can't we forgive others? It is very difficult to forgive when we have been harmed, but the price we pay for not forgiving is far greater. The negative effects of holding grudges and nursing contempt, anger, and all the other negative and damaging emotions are far more destructive than simply letting go. The old cliché "Let go and let God" really is important to detoxifying your life of unhealthy relationships.

Love heals toxic relationships. When you start to see people the way God sees them, you will begin to experience the cleansing, refreshing spirit of his love. God's Spirit of love produces health, joy, and peace. It isn't easy, but it is the only way to go. When you start living this way, you will experience the blessings of God.

Our preconceived notions of people often determine the responses we will get. This is true whether we think the best or the worst. For example, if you see people suspiciously, they will not respond positively to you and you will find something to warrant your suspicion.

A story is told of a teacher back in 1965 who had the best of intentions. She was a kind, elderly woman who received a teaching position in one of the roughest schools in New York City. On the first day of school, the principal gave her a list of students with numbers next to each name. The teacher looked up and down at this list of names and corresponding numbers and knew that she had been entrusted with the brightest students in the school. Throughout the year, her class did exceptionally well academically. At the end-of-the-year awards ceremony for all the students and faculty at the school, the principal called her forward. She had received the Outstanding Teacher of the Year award.

The principal introduced her saying, "Miss Harris accepted the position as our sixth-grade teacher in November of this year. She was the third teacher to accept the challenge. The other two just couldn't work under the conditions. Not only did she get through the year, but she miraculously brought the students to the top of their class academically."

She accepted the applause and the plaque. She told the audience, "I knew I couldn't fail. They were all so bright. I never, in all my years of teaching, ever had a class filled with smarter children. When I saw their IQs, I was confused about why the other teachers had a problem."

After the speech, the principal went over to her and asked, "Where did you get IQs of the students?"

"You gave them to me on the first day of class," she replied.

"No," responded the principal, "I gave you their locker numbers."

For me, the message through the years has been "you find what you're looking for." When it comes to relationships, how you see people will determine how they respond to you. If you treat people with respect, they respond in a respectful way. If you treat them contemptuously, sarcasm and rudeness come in return. The teacher expected her students to be the best and she got the best in return.

Our perceptions greatly determine what kind of relationships we have and how toxic they are. The Academy Award–winning movie *Life Is Beautiful* develops this theme in the most incongruous conditions. The setting is Nazi Germany. A father and his five-year-old son are sent to a concentration camp. The father, in an attempt to make the experience tolerable for his son, tells him the entire thing is a contest in which the winner gets a real army tank. The boy loved tanks. The father altered the child's perception of the circumstances so that he would not loose his will to live. In the eyes of the child, everything the Gestapo did, fueled by the words of his father, was to make all the children lose. The one who could go the distance would win. The movie ends when an American tank comes around the corner and picks up the boy, who declares, "It is true! There is a tank. I won, I won, I won!"

You can win against the most unbelievable odds. Foes will turn into friends, toxic relationships will be transformed into nourishing ones, and you will see people through the eyes of God. Possibility Living follows Christ's command, "Love one another" (John 13:34).

Step 3: Maintain Healthy Boundaries

At times, it is necessary to set a boundary between yourself and a toxic person. Some toxic people will defy all your attempts to get them to respond positively. No matter what you offer them in word, thought, or deed, you always get the same garbage back. We must remember that the command of Christ is to "love" them—not to live with them, but to visit them, feed them, and clothe them. "Whatever you do for one of the least for these, you do for me" (Matt. 25:45).

"The least of these" are often the people we may mistakenly believe have no needs. Too often we associate need with money and physical comforts, while the greatest need of all is the need of love. The people who refuse to accept our love are the ones from whom we need protection. They suck everything in and give nothing back. They are spiritually dead. They may have the trappings of a spiritual life, but without love they are nothing more than a noisy gong or a clanging symbol. They need love the most.

However, only a few can give love to them without getting hurt in the process. It takes a person with a strong spiritual foundation and solid boundaries. Without God's transforming power in their lives, the toxic people around you will become all the more toxic. You become ill instead of the ill becoming well. If you believe you are ready to reach out and care for the emotional "least of these" or if you are in a situation where you do not feel you have any other choice, then be certain that you have solid boundaries.

Boundaries are fences with gates, more secure than just lines drawn in the sand. A fence keeps livestock in a certain area that's safe. Gates allow the animals to go into other areas. Imagine only drawing lines in the sand and telling livestock not to cross them.

Boundaries must be set in emotional concrete, not emotional sand. If your boundaries are in sand, you cannot expect to minister to the needy without getting hurt. You need to know yourself and your boundaries. They must be firm, solid, and unmovable. This will enable us to begin the service of loving the loveless.

Emotions are unpredictable. Although you cannot control emotions, you can control actions. When setting boundaries, it is crucial to follow reason rather than emotion. Anger, fear, frustration, hope, joy, peace, and goodness are all emotions that enrich life. The Holy Spirit enhances life like salt enhances flavor and light enhances vision. When the Holy Spirit of God comes upon you, the presence of the peace of God overwhelms your soul and your heart. Emotions you never knew you had will well within. You will begin to feel pain. You'll begin to feel joy again. As you begin to experience life and the reality of God's goodness, Possibility Living will embrace you. The Holy Spirit empowers us to feel emotions, but also to use the mind of Christ to set boundaries.

We need more than our own strength to set boundaries. Setting and maintaining boundaries is a big job in our lives. Let me give you an illustration. We have more than one vacuum in our home. With four kids, we have two different vacuums to cleanup different messes. One of our vacuums is a small cordless one that runs on a battery. If the dirt you have to clean up requires more than a few minutes of vacuum power, you are out of luck. The battery only lasts a few minutes and then the power is gone. If you have a lot of dirt, then it's time to bring out the larger vacuum. You plug it in, turn it on, and it will continue to vacuum as long as you keep it plugged in and turned on. It'll level a mountain of dirt. What's the difference between the two? One's plugged into a source that will not end, while the other is completely dependent upon its own power.

Without the Holy Spirit, without understanding who God is, without realizing that God wants to help you feel again and be in control of your life, you're on your own. Your out-of-control feelings will take over. Your reason will capitulate. And your boundaries will wash away like sand castles disappearing under the ocean's waves. Toxic people will crash into your life and drain all your energy and emotions unless the Holy Spirit helps you draw firm boundaries with the mind of Christ. Setting firm boundaries is knowing what you believe and then sticking to your convictions.

Follow your convictions, not the crowd. As I mentioned earlier, it is very easy to be sucked into the crowd. It is natural. But we are not just physical beings; we are spiritual beings on a human journey. We follow our God-given human potential, our convictions, our calling, and our destiny.

Standing out in a crowd because of our convictions is never fun. People want us to be the same as they are. When you stand out, you become a light shining on their spiritual failure. Their toxic behavior becomes ever more clear as you continue to shine. If they can put your light out by putting you back in your place, then the light that shines on their sickness goes out and it is easier for them to continue in denial.

We are left then with this choice: immediate popularity or ultimate respect. The immediate gratification of popularity is very tempting, especially in our fast-paced world. Waiting for anything goes against the grain. "Lord, Give me patience, and give it to me right *now!*" is a common prayer. It's a sign of the times. But good things come to those who wait. "Those who wait on the Lord shall renew their strength; they shall mount up with wings like eagles, they shall run and not be weary, they shall walk and not faint" (Isa. 40:31).

If you hold on to your spiritual boundaries while seeking ultimate respect, you will be rewarded with something far more valuable than the weeds of popularity. Anyone who has ever planted a garden will testify to the fact that the first plants to sprout from newly sown soil will not be the flowers or vegetables, but weeds. They come first. The fruit of a garden takes hard work and patience. It is the same with detoxifying our relationships.

CONCLUSION

A word for the wise: Choose your battles wisely. Relationships usually boil down to two kinds of interaction: adult–child or adult–adult. When you decide to have an adult–adult relationship with someone, it is a difficult transition. Everyone begins life with child–adult relationships. However, as we mature, we need to change all our relationships to adult–adult.

Some employers treat their employees like children. Often aggressive people treat others like children. The toughest relationships in this regard are with parents. Most parents do not know how to let their children grow up or how to have an adult–adult relationship with them. When you are ready to grow up and begin this new understanding and communication system of adult–adult, you will go through a very difficult transition. It will probably begin with a battle. So choose your battles wisely. Stand firm. Adult–adult relationships move beyond childish behavior to healthy, mature interaction.

Begin by choosing a battle you cannot lose. This will require wisdom. Be sure to pray about it first. Enter into it logically and know that as you travel through the valley of change you will be on the path to wellness and wholeness. As you detoxify your relationships, you will be moving from adult–child relationships to adult–adult ones.

We have spent a lifetime creating the relationships we now have. If they are healthy ones, they are nourishing, rewarding, and respectful in an adult–adult way. As for the toxic relationships, they are disabling, demeaning, and adult–child. If you find yourself today in a negative relationship, choose the Possibility Living way of making the right choice to detoxify your negative relationships, grow up, and put away your childish ways. It will not be simple or painless, but it is the best thing you can do, and it will add years to your life and life to those years.

CHAPTER 10

DETOXIFY YOUR STRESS

Dr. Douglas Di Siena

Possibility Living helps us to make the right choices about diet, health, fitness, lifestyle, thought patterns, relationships, and spirituality. Making the wrong choices in these areas of our lives creates stress.

Stress has been around since the beginning of time. In fact, stress is first mentioned in Genesis. After making a wrong choice and hiding from his Creator, Adam reveals his stress, "I heard you in the garden, and I was afraid because I was naked; so I hid" (Gen. 3:10). Proverbs speaks about the mind-body connection as it relates to stress: "A heart at peace gives life to the body, but envy rots the bones" (Prov. 14:30). In the Sermon on the Mount (Matt. 5–7), Christ mentions the issue of worry (stress) six times. Toxic stress affects our body, mind, and spirit.

Everyone deals with stress constantly. Research has produced volumes of information on stress, both the positive and the negative kinds. Positive stress keeps our bodies functioning at an optimum level producing what God has called us to do, while toxic stress tears us down, hurts, injures, and belittles us. As scientists are discovering, stress can have a tremendous negative impact on our bodies, especially on our immune and endocrine systems.

The term "stressed" was first used by Dr. Hans Sele back in the 1930s. However, it wasn't until recently that we began to understand the impact of stress and its toxic effects. As part of our new patient package, my clinic makes a point of asking about lifestyle issues. Most of our patients indicate that they have very stressful lifestyles. Stress seems to be a growing epidemic in our culture.

THE NEGATIVE IMPACT OF STRESS ON OUR LIVES

We might define stress as a strain or force exerted on our body and mind. The mind and body then call on energy reserves to oppose or resist the force. The continual presence of force and counterforce creates tension, which is the hallmark of a stressful life. This tension greatly inhibits our ability to respond appropriately to changes in life, which in turn increases the likelihood of illness.

Within our bodies are two parts of the autonomic (automatic) nervous system—the parasympathetic and the sympathetic. In a calm and relaxed state—the opposite of stress—the parasympathetic part of our nervous system is in control. When we are relaxed, our bodies provide maximum healing energy for repair, regeneration, and renewal. In this state, our hands are warm and all of our basic functions like blood pressure, pulse, and respiration are at their slowest. We are also at our most creative. We feel more, smell more, and can sense more.

The sympathetic nervous system is designed to take over in times of perceived extreme danger. The sympathetic nervous system puts everything on red alert. The mind perceives a threat and prepares the body to fight or to run. In this crisis mode, everything in our bodies that was resting now moves into high gear. Our bodies produce a massive quantity of adrenaline, our heart rate is racing, and our hands are cold as a result of the diversion of blood from the metabolic and detoxing organs to skeletal muscles, the heart, and the lungs. In short, everything in us is fueled for "fight or flight."

The sympathetic nervous system also instructs our adrenal system to produce adrenaline and many other stress hormones, including cortisol. Adrenaline raises cortisol levels, which, in turn, elevate blood-sugar levels and the chemical cycle continues. God has designed all of this as a survival mechanism. The stress cycle is meant to save our lives in times of impending danger. However, far too many of us spend too much time in this fight-or-flight response mode when we are not facing a physical threat. We move into this mode as the result of some perceived fear, yet even though we are afraid, we put up a façade of trying to act relaxed.

Imagine accelerating a car's speed to 55 m.p.h. and then putting it on cruise control. Once the cruise control is set, we then take the car out of gear. As the car senses a decrease in speed, it signals to the accelerator to speed up, which is of no use because the car will continue to slow down no matter how much the car's accelerator tries otherwise. This is analogous to what is going on in our body when we are under stress. We perceive impending danger and our sympathetic nervous system begins to speed up all of our body's functions, while on the outside we are trying hard to look calm and relaxed. We are getting signals from the brain that danger is present, yet the body is not responding. High levels of fear and worry send the body into overdrive, severely taxing our systems. Imagine living your day-to-day life in this state.

I see many patients who operate in this crisislike state most of the time. Our bodies were created to spend most of their time in the parasympathetic mode, with the rare occasions when we get a turbo boost from the sympathetic nervous system. Since our bodies have only a finite amount of energy, if we use our energy to cope with stress much of the time, then the energy our bodies need for repair and maintenance—healing—is diminished.

STRESS CAUSES DISEASE

When we think of stress-caused disease, the first one most people think about is high blood pressure. We have heard from so many, "You are making my blood pressure go up." The truth is that many cases of high blood pressure are a result of toxic stress. Most cases of asymptomatic high blood pressure (with no or minimal symptoms) are a result of lifestyle choices having to do with diet, exercise, and stress. Once again, stress magnifies any preexisting condition. For example, if individuals make the wrong diet choices and then add stress to the equation, high blood pressure could well be the next condition they encounter.

Johns Hopkins School of Medicine did a study based on forty years of prospective data and reported psychological factors (emotional stress) as predictors of five disease states.[1] These psychological factors were these:

1. response to stress with hopelessness

2. bottling up emotions or having impaired emotional outlets

3. perceived lack of closeness with one or both parents

Stress is a physical response of the nervous system to a perceived impending danger. Unfortunately, most of us feel stress not as a physical state, but an emotional state. This confuses the nervous system and diminishes the brain's ability to correlate and integrate the various bodily processes for optimal function. When our bodies are not optimally functioning, it becomes difficult for us to readily respond to an ever changing environment.

If you are living in the fight-or-flight syndrome, under extreme stress, you need to make a positive, constructive change in your lifestyle. Particular stressful events are often unavoidable—the loss of a loved one, being laid off from work, starting a new job, or coping with an unexpected financial crisis. Living with chronic, ongoing stress, however, is avoidable. In Possibility Living, you have the God-given ability to make right choices. Too much stress signals the need for a change.

MY STRESS SIGNAL

In June 1986, I left a group practice to start a solo private practice. As my practice grew, so did the length of time patients had to wait to see me. When I noticed people were waiting for me, I begin to feel tension. My hands would turn cold, and all of those stress hormones would start to flood my system. I found myself worrying about the patient in the reception room while I was working with another patient. Due to being stressed out, I wasn't treating each patient with the attention I should have.

As a result, I began to lose that special connection with my patients that I had enjoyed previously. I lost that feeling of knowing exactly what was wrong with the patient. Both what to do and what to say became a conscious effort, whereas before my heightened stress levels everything seemed to just flow. In short, I felt as if I had lost the gift of really helping people through my practice. I was in a slump. My fatigue increased along with my stress. The toxic effects of stress invaded my life, my practice, and my relationships. I had to make a choice.

At a professional meeting, I met a dynamic colleague, Dr. Ron Oberstein, who listened to my plight and gave me two wise insights for handling stress. Ron said that a practice could only grow from the inside. He explained the same philosophy for business as for life. He reiterated the A.D.I.O. principle. Then he challenged me with this wisdom:

1. *Respond to stress with love not fear.* Stressors exist all around us— a traffic jam, a bounced check, an angry store clerk, or a demanding boss. We can fear them, or simply love others and ourselves. We have the choice.

2. *Focus on the present.* Don't worry about the future. Dr. Oberstein advised me to give every patient an adjustment with that something extra called love. Instead of worrying about who was waiting to see me next, I needed to completely focus my attention to the person I was with at that moment. He challenged me to try to see God in every single person I saw.

Dr. Oberstein wasn't telling me anything that hadn't already been revealed by Jesus. Jesus said it this way:

So don't worry about having enough food or drink or clothing. Why be like the pagans who are so deeply concerned about these things? Your heavenly Father already knows all your needs, and he will give you all you need from day to day if you live for him and make the Kingdom of God your primary concern. So don't worry about tomorrow, for tomorrow will bring its own worries. Today's trouble is enough for today.

Matthew 6:31–34, NLT

My practice doubled within a month of that meeting. People were seeing results. Today, I must say that, with a few managerial exceptions, my practice is a stress-free environment. People tell me they feel the love as they enter into the office. Paradoxically, I spend less time with each patient, yet they get all that I have, and we have a more meaningful exchange. I now can enjoy the time spent with each one of my patients.

HOW MUCH STRESS IS TOO MUCH?

Toxic stress breaks down our bodies and wreaks havoc on our souls and spirits. When we go into stress overload, we are saturated at every moment with stress that's producing the fight-or-flight syndrome in our bodies.

I describe this phenomenon as the saturation effect. It is very much like the experiment many of us did in chemistry lab in which we took a beaker of pure water and added sugar, one teaspoon at a time, until the water reached its saturation level. The water looks perfectly clear to the eye; however, as it approaches its saturation capacity, even the tiniest additional particle of sugar cannot get dissolved and turns the entire beaker cloudy.

Stress functions in a similar way. Our bodies were created to tolerate a certain amount of stress on a daily basis. However, when we get to the point where we are at our limit, any small amount of additional stress could destabilize us. For example, dad pulls into the driveway after a stressful day at work and sees his son's bike blocking his route to the garage. Instead of getting out of the car, moving the bike, and driving calmly into the garage, he storms into the house and yells at his son in a fit of rage. Normally that bike in the driveway would not have been a big deal, but because of stress his world has been destabilized by that "extra grain of sugar" added to the mix of his day. He's stressed out, over the edge, and toxic to himself and others.

We have all seen people whose world is unstable. They are short-sighted, short-tempered, and short on apologies. Paradoxically, they cause more stress for themselves and others instead of making right choices to reduce their stress. Their stress infects the people around them, causing everyone to have to handle extra stress. Possibility Living chooses to handle stress positively instead of toxically.

YOUR PERSONAL STRESS TEST

Take a moment to assess your current stress level with the following stress test.[2] Mark the events below that you have recently experienced. Then add up the mean values for the events you marked to find your total.

HOLMES-RAHE SOCIAL SCALE OF STRESS

Mean value	Description of stressor
100	Death of spouse
73	Divorce
65	Marital separation
63	Jail term
63	Death of close family member
53	Personal injury or illness
50	Marriage
47	Fired at work
45	Marriage reconciliation
45	Retirement
44	Change in health of family member
40	Pregnancy
39	Sex difficulties
39	Gain of a new family member

39	Business readjustment
38	Change in financial state
37	Death of close friend
36	Change to different line of work
35	Change in the number of arguments with wife
31	Mortgage over 35% of your net income*
30	Foreclosure of mortgage
29	Change in responsibilities at work
29	Son or daughter leaving home
29	Trouble with in-laws
28	Outstanding personal achievement

The developers of this scale, Drs. Rahe and Holmes, believe that those who have a cumulative score of greater than 300, have an 80 percent chance of developing a serious illness with in one year.

When is your stress too much? If you fail to handle your stress, you will notice that you are putting yourself and everyone around you in a constant fight-or-flight mode. In other words, you are stressed out and everyone around you is stressed by your stress. Instead of living in toxicity and exposing your body and mind to disease, you can choose to take steps to reduce your stress, react positively instead of negatively, and create a more relaxed and enjoyable environment for yourself and others. Here's how to reduce your stress.

POSSIBILITY LIVING STEPS TOWARD REDUCING YOUR STRESS

Become God-Centered, Instead of Crisis-Centered

God is aware of all our needs even before we are. He knows the numbers of hairs on our head. When we live a God-centered life, by default we move away from being self-centered. God has tomorrow under control; we don't have to worry about it. He is the source of all wisdom and thus we aren't alone in handling our crises.

---

*The original test for 1967 read "Mortgage over $10,000.

I once heard that our ability to live in the present tense determines the degree to which we are sane. If we stay God-centered, we must be in the present moment. He is the God of the now. The past is forgiven. The future belongs in his hands. The life we have to live is only in the now. In the present moment, there is no stress about yesterday or about tomorrow. There is only now.

In the present moment, God is with us. Christ promised, "And be sure of this: I am with you always, even to the end of the age" (Matt. 28:20, NLT). Knowing that God is love (1 John 4:8), we can be assured that in the present moment, one reality exists—love. Love comes from *above down*. In the toxin-free and stress-free environment of his love, there is only peace and the ability to maximize all healing. When we are in a stressful state, we have to ask ourselves, are we being self-centered or God-centered?

Focus Your Mind on the Positive

When stressed, we are tempted to focus on the negatives. We find ourselves looking for what can go wrong. Stress often causes us to worry about the unknowns.

The apostle Paul knew how to handle stress. He wrote:

> Rejoice in the Lord always. I will say it again: Rejoice! Let your gentleness be evident to all. The Lord is near. Do not be anxious about anything, but in everything, by prayer and petition, with thanksgiving, present your requests to God. And the peace of God, which transcends all understanding, will guard your hearts and your minds in Christ Jesus. Finally, brothers, whatever is true, whatever is noble, whatever is right, whatever is pure, whatever is lovely, whatever is admirable—if anything is excellent or praiseworthy—think about such things.
>
> Philippians 4:4–8

Paul recognizes that the best way to handle stress is to think about the positives and to give the negatives to God. The Bible counsels us,

"Give all your worries and cares to God, for he cares about what happens to you" (1 Pet. 5:7, NLT).

Remember that it's not necessarily just the stress—it's what you think about the stress that creates the toxicity. Paul has great wisdom for us: "I know what it is to be in need, and I know what it is to have plenty. I have learned the secret of being content in any and every situation, whether well fed or hungry, whether living in plenty or in want" (Phil. 4:12). He wrote this text while chained in what must have been a very repulsive Roman prison.

Paul helps us understand how we can choose not to be victims in most circumstances and know that joy is not circumstantial. But joy, as with all the fruits of the Spirit, comes from *above down*, flows *inside* of us, then *out* to others.

Turn Your Stress into Strength with Optimism

How toxic your stress becomes is determined by how you feel about the stress you are enduring. You can endure stress with either an optimistic or a pessimistic attitude. You can decide to grow stronger as a result of your stress or allow your stress to weaken and debilitate you. You can choose hope over despair. The optimistic person views stress as an opportunity to grow stronger, while the pessimist sees stress as a crisis draining away strength. How do you view your stress?

Keep Praying Rather Than Fighting against Stress

Although we all face struggles in life, some have the ability to cope better than others. Some handle stress by getting angry and fighting against it. Others make the right choice to cope positively. Coping with your stress is greatly enhanced through

- staying connected with God
- staying connected with others

A recent study examined prayer as a direct coping mechanism for those patients awaiting cardiac surgery. Researchers watched one hundred patients and studied their coping ability with prayer. Ninety-six patients said that they used prayer as a coping mechanism to reduce the stress. Of the four who did not pray, two had people who were praying for them. Ninety-seven of the one hundred patients felt that prayer had a positive influence on their stress levels. Seventy of these subjects gave it the highest possible rating on the Helpfulness of Prayer Scale. The study concluded that patients can learn to cope with the stress by being taught and encouraged to pray.[3]

It's almost impossible to cope with anything when you are isolated and alone. God loves and supports. Friends can give you the support and strength you need to go on. Staying connected to God and friends will give you the strength to cope with stress.

Keep a Journal to Help You Release Your Stress

Writing in a diary or journal about your stressful situations will help you release inner tensions and negative emotions. Holding onto those toxic, stressful feelings can cause that fight-or-flight syndrome to work overtime in your body.

A study published in the *Journal of the American Medical Association* demonstrates that keeping a journal and writing about past stressful events, such as a death of a spouse, helps reduce stress levels significantly.[4] The study revealed the following:

1. Patients with chronic conditions seemed to improve.

2. Asthmatics' lung capacities improved in only about two weeks.

3. Arthritis patients improved.

A wonderful book I recommend to anybody in the battle to regain health is called *Anatomy of an Illness*, by Norman Cousins. The book illustrates the real recovery of a person who was successful in radically changing his illness paradigm.

In 1976, Norman Cousins "cured" himself of an illness. He reasoned that if negative emotions can have a negative impact on his health, then positive feelings could only help his body recover. Cousins decided that while he was in a bed, sick and suffering, he would take responsibility for his attitude and thus his health. He ordered a film projector and started to watch movies that would make him not just giggle, but really laugh. He loved to watch old slapstick movies and funny television shows, and he even had those close to him read him humorous stories. He wrote, "I made a discovery that ten minutes of belly laughter had an anesthetic effect that would give me at least two hours of pain-free sleep."

He requested that his doctors start to reduce his levels of medication and put him on high levels of vitamin C. Cousins's doctors decided to do some laboratory blood tests to determine the reality of his improvement with his self-prescribed laughter therapy. They found that after each one of his laughter sessions, his sedimentation rates (a very sensitive test used to measure most inflammatory disease states) had lowered.

Many studies have followed to demonstrate that the two major immune-lowering hormones released as a result of stress (epinephrine and cortisol) are lowered when people were subjected to comedy. Biblical wisdom reveals, "A happy heart makes the face cheerful, but heartache crushes the spirit" (Prov 15:13, NIV) and "A cheerful heart is good medicine, but a broken spirit saps a person's strength" (Prov. 17:22).

Dr. Gary Swartz teaches the "ACE" method of dealing with stress.[5]

- Attend to situations and feelings. Don't bury or hide your feelings—face them.

- Connect to those feelings. Keep in touch with what you are feeling.

- Express your feelings appropriately. Cry or laugh. Rejoice or grieve. Let your feelings out in a way that doesn't harm you or others.

Stress is toxic only when we lose hope in our future. As with so many other issues, it is what we do with what we are given that makes the difference. We live in a world that seems to be forever stressful, so we must become more conscious about how we think, feel, and respond to stress.

We have explored natural, positive steps you can take to cope with and reduce your stress. You can't avoid stress, but you don't have to carry it with you. Yesterday's problems coupled with tomorrow's worry can enslave your present in unbearable stress. *Refuse to live in toxic stress.*

Possibility Living offers the right choices for handling stress:

- Become God-centered.

- Focus on what's positive.

- Find strength in hope and optimism.

- Keep connected through prayer.

- Keep connected through healthy relationships with others.

- Keep a journal.

- Laugh a lot.

- ACE your feelings.

CHAPTER 11

DETOXIFY YOUR HABITS

Dr. Robert A. Schuller

Habits can be either good or bad. Are all of the habits you have positive, healthy, and rewarding? Or are any of them negative, toxic, and, destructive? Possibility Living makes the choice to turn negative habits into positive ones. For example, if you can turn the habit of smoking into the habit of exercise, the resulting physical benefits will make a remarkable difference in adding years to your life and life to those years. Trade donuts for apples, booze for water, hate for love, and drug stores for health food stores, and then only God will be able to measure the quantity of improvement.

The thought of changing old, comfortable habits, as damaging as they may be, is frightening. Change is not something we enjoy doing. Often we will choose a pill instead of the necessary lifestyle changes. Anything is better than having to give up a good old buddy. The longer we have had the negative behavior, the harder it is to give it up.

In 1996, I interviewed Dr. Edward Taub on the topic of smoking. His smoking cessation program has a 97 percent success rate. In his program, he leads his patients through the steps that give them the ability to quit. His success begins with a pledge to God: "I swear to God to quit!" Many people have a problem making that pledge. That pledge, however, determines the success of the program. Many who are afraid to make that commitment are held back by their "nicotine-drenched thoughts." The physical addiction has become overlaid with a psychological addiction to nicotine.

The physical addiction to the nicotine actually lasts only seventy-two hours. This means that if a smoker can go three days without a cigarette or another nicotine source, he or she will be completely free of the chemical addiction. Why is it that so many smokers go back after a week or two or three? The answer lies in the nicotine-drenched thoughts that keep a smoker hooked for what can be months or even years. Therefore, any quality smoking cessation program requires a whole-person program. Dr. Edward Taub offers the following seven steps to quitting once and for all. One week prior to actually stopping, do the following:

1. Smoke only outside. Put ashes and butts in the same glass jar. Don't clean it out—just add to it for seven days.

2. Take a brisk ten-minute walk every day.

3. Pray to God to help you every day.

4. Keep telling your friends, family, and associates what you are going to do. Count down to the day you quit.

5. Swear to God never to smoke again.

6. Drink at least eight glasses of water a day (other beverages do not count).

7. Take a good multiple vitamin along with your antioxidants: vitamin C, 1500 mg.; vitamin E, 400 IU; and beta-carotene, 15,000 IU.

Thousands of people have quit with this method. You can too. If you want to add years to your life and life to those years and you smoke, you need to quit.

I started with the example of smoking, but other habits also suck life out of us. Alcohol, when abused, destroys lives, families, and careers. I say "when abused" because studies show red wine has some protective benefits against heart disease. I am also aware that alcohol should never be combined with any other medication, especially over-the-counter painkillers (please note that the FDA warns against this, as it could be life-threatening).

One of my books is entitled *Dump Your Hang-ups Without Dumping Them on Others.* In this book, I share a twelve-step approach to dumping our bad habits and addictions without dumping them on our families, friends, and associates. Toxic habits and hang-ups include compulsive eating, alcohol abuse, drug abuse, smoking, sexual addictions, and other immoral behavior. I believe that the twelve-step approach is the best way to deal with our negative, self-destructive behavior. I follow the same steps that have been used by Alcoholics Anonymous for years. They have been proven over and over again to be a very effective means of behavior modification. I have slightly changed the original twelve steps of Alcoholics Anonymous to ones broader in scope so they may be applied to more than alcohol consumption.

TWELVE STEPS FOR BREAKING TOXIC HABITS

1. I will admit that I am powerless over my habit or hang-up and that my life is unmanageable.

2. I will acknowledge that God is greater than I and that he can bring restoration to my life.

3. I will turn my life over to God.

4. I will make a searching and fearless moral inventory of myself.

5. I will admit to God, myself, and another human being the exact nature of my wrongs.

6. I will make myself entirely ready to have God remove any defects from my character and bring about the necessary changes in my life.

7. I will humbly ask God to remove my shortcomings.

8. I will make a list of the people I have harmed by my past behavior and become willing to make amends.

9. Wherever possible, I will make direct amends to the people my behavior has harmed.

10. I will continue to take personal inventory of my life on a regular basis and promptly admit it when I do something wrong or lapse back into old behavior patterns.

11. I will seek to know more of God.

12. I will seek to carry to others the glorious message of the possibility of a spiritual awakening.

These steps have had a profound positive impact on the lives of countless people. Only God knows how many lives they have saved.

There is a statement that summarizes the first three steps, which are the most critical. It says, "I can't, He can, Let Him." Everyone has an "Achilles' heel"—a vulnerable spot that, if aggravated, can really send a person plummeting into old habits, anger, depression, or hopelessness. You may not have learned to manage those vulnerabilities. And when outside stresses hit, they can become like millstones tied to your neck, pulling you with great force down to rock bottom.

One member of my congregation has a wonderful testimony about how he began coming to our church. He was watching television in his bedroom on a Sunday morning. As he surfed through the channels, he saw my father. Curiosity stopped him. He listened. It was the beginning of a new life for him, at age thirty-five. There he was in his bathrobe holding a beer. It was only ten o'clock in the morning. Behind him, a naked woman was sleeping beneath the sheets. He didn't even know her last name. He had no children and no steady job. He didn't know where he was going with his life. That morning he fell on his knees and prayed. And when he did, he began a new life.

There are many people, perhaps including you, who are in the same place that my friend was before that redemptive day. Maybe you have a family you love or a steady job, but you have shortcomings. Maybe those shortcomings are rooted in childhood problems that keep you from being everything that God intended you to be. Maybe those shortcomings are simply bad choices you have made. But no matter why they are there, those shortcomings are hindering you from becoming everything that God has intended you to be. This doesn't mean that you are a bad person. You just have a few toxic habits. Today you can choose to be a good person en route to becoming a better person by deciding to turn those toxic habits into positive ones.

You can transform any toxic habits, whatever they may be, by following the principles offered in the following steps.

Step 1: Recognize That You Are Powerless

When we recognize that we are powerless, we actually receive power. This is a tremendous paradox, but it really is true. What is power? When we look at various forms of power, we see the oldest, most primitive form of power—the power of violence. I believe that this is the weakest form of power, and yet it is one that is so hastily embraced.

As children, most of us were pushed around at one time or another by somebody bigger or more daring than ourselves. It is frightening, but today many teens have moved from using fists to using weapons. Teens today must fear for their lives when they go to school. Is aggression really a form of strength? It takes a lot more guts for someone to back down than to pull a trigger. It takes a lot more self-discipline to admit when we are wrong than it does to fight. Yet, it isn't only teens who face this challenge. Many adults take their anger out on others, both physically and verbally. Violence, in any form, is a weak kind of power. But what is real power?

One of the greatest forms of power is knowledge. I don't mean intellectual knowledge. One of the greatest forms of power lies in the knowledge that we are, in ourselves, powerless. We come to understand that we cannot do it alone. As the original First Step states, "We must admit that we are powerless over the effects of our shortcomings;

that our lives have become unmanageable." Real power comes from the One who has all power, from the One who has the greatest knowledge. God is the One who has been to the future and back.

Step 2: Recognize God's Power

In the Bible, St. Paul writes, "For it is God who works in you, both to will and to act according to His good purpose" (Phil. 2:13). It is God who restores us to wholeness.

David McQuay, a newspaper columnist for the *Orange County Register*, a local newspaper, recently passed away from cancer. In one of his last articles, he wrote about some profound discoveries. An excerpt reads as follows:

> The priest came and gave me Communion at my hospital bed. I felt a warmth around my head. He prayed a spontaneous prayer, and I felt transformed. I'm still trying to understand what happened. I grew up Catholic and went to Catholic school for twelve years. I was humiliated by nuns, hated the folk-rock mass, disagreed with Rome on issues, and after graduating from high school, I left the church. I went to church for weddings and funerals. But then, at forty, death approached my door. A priest at St. Joseph's Hospital was in the doorway. I said, "Father, I need Communion." On Monday, the priest arrived and gave me Communion and said another prayer. He laid his hands on my stomach and prayed as he had before. And I felt a state of bliss. Other remarkable things happened. My mother had an unusual spiritual experience while praying for me that week. Four people I had not talked with for nine years called me one day, wishing me well. So here is what I think happened. Call it God, or love. Maybe it's the same thing. But a wave of energy moved through this priest, who uttered the most beautiful prayer I've ever heard. I told a doctor about my experience. He said, "When a patient has a spiritual awakening, he or she gets better." I still have cancer. But what the priest did most of all

was remove my fears and anxieties, like a surgeon removing a tumor. And he pumped the blood of faith into me.[1]

You may be feeling that there is no hope and the future holds nothing but pain, grief, and fear. The truth is, however, when you recognize your powerlessness and look into the face of God, you will realize his power. Faith will pump through you and you will feel the presence of a living God and become empowered.

How do you do this? How do you see the face of God and receive the power to overcome the struggles and the challenges of every single day? The answer is very simple. Pray.

> *I got up early one morning, not long ago, intending to rush right into the day.*
> *I had much to accomplish before sundown. I didn't have time to pray.*
> *Problems tumbled about me. Each task became more difficult to tackle.*
> *I thought, "Why isn't God helping me?"*
> *Then quite unexpected and sudden, I sensed the response, "You didn't ask."*

Step 3: Let Go and Let God

> *I tried to come into God's presence,*
> *I used all my keys at the lock,*
> *God gently and lovingly chided,*
> *"My child, you didn't knock."*

I know a mother who had been praying for her eight-year-old son, Bobby. The doctors had diagnosed Bobby with cancer and there was nothing they could do for him. One day, she came to Bobby and said, "Bobby, if you could have anything you wanted, what would it be?" And he responded, "Mommy, I want to be a fireman." She didn't know how to respond. After giving it some thought, she decided to talk to the local fire chief. She said to him, "Sir, my son has only a few weeks, maybe a couple of months, to live. It is his dying wish to become a fireman. Is there anything you can do?"

To her shock, the chief responded, "Yes, there is. Wait here just a minute." He walked over and talked to some of the other firemen. He then told the mother what they would do. The next day a group from the fire department went to the hospital. Once there, they measured Bobby's feet, height, and head. A few days later they returned with a special pair of overalls, a special coat, a special hat, and a special pair of boots custom made for little Bobby. They fit perfectly. The firemen told Bobby that the next day he felt up to it, he should come down to the station.

A few days later, Bobby was feeling unusually well. His mother brought him to the fire station and he spent the entire day with his new friends. He wore his new uniform and rode on the fire engine. He sounded the siren. He stood next to them and watched from a distance as they performed various duties. For that entire day, he was "Fireman Bobby."

A few weeks later, Bobby's health degenerated. The nurse called up the fire chief and said, "Chief, it doesn't look like Bobby will make it through the night. We just thought you'd like to know." The chief had become especially fond of his new friend. The chief responded, "Would you please tell all of your patients not to worry. In a few minutes, they will see some lights and see some things going on, but tell them it's okay. Would you please do that for me?" She agreed.

A few minutes later, the sirens sounded, the lights flashed, and a line of trucks paraded down the street and pulled right in front of Bobby's room. The parade ended. Firemen poured from the vehicles. A ladder truck hoisted a ladder up to Bobby's third-floor window, and the chief climbed up the ladder and through the window and stood at Bobby's side. Bobby looked at the chief. Then he said, "Chief, am I really a fireman?" The chief responded, "The best we've ever had."

Some of you today are looking to God and saying. "God, am I really powerful through you?" And God is saying, "I have come that you might have life, and have it abundantly. I have come to bring you joy and goodness and hope. You are the finest."

Say this prayer, again and again, "Not my will, O Lord, but yours be done." Then allow the Spirit of God to lead you into an act of kindness. It may seem to be something little, but you won't believe what God can do with a just a little. It doesn't take much.

One Christmas, several years ago, my father was shopping on the streets of Laguna Beach, California, when he noticed the meter maid coming down the street writing tickets for cars in expired spaces. He watched for a moment then thought to himself, "All these poor people have to pay these fines on Christmas. What a shame." He got an idea. He went into a store and changed some dollar bills for a bunch of dimes, nickels, and quarters. He started walking the streets, depositing coins in every expired meter. Most of the car owners never knew that they were spared a traffic ticket, but Dad knew and God knew. Give a little kindness to someone and feel the power of God flow through you.

How do we detox our habits?

1. Recognize our powerlessness.

2. Recognize God's power.

3. Let go and let God.

If you implement these first three steps in your life with dedication and commitment, you are building a foundation that is essential for tackling the next steps.

The next two steps are, in my opinion, the most difficult of the twelve steps. However, they are imperative if you want to gain the skills that will lead to better living.

Step 4: Make a Fearless Moral Inventory of Yourself

Lamentations 3:40 reads, "Let us examine our ways and test them and then let us return to the Lord." As children, we were all raised in imperfect families. As parents, we are all raising imperfect children. We have challenges as we guide our children to maturity. Likewise, children have challenges and difficulties that they face every day. Because of this, the family and the home face tremendous stress.

I remember when my first daughter was born. At one point during the first week she was home, my wife and I decided we'd go out and get an ice cream cone together, just the two of us. It seemed a nice, simple thing to do. We put on our sweaters, and just as we were ready to get into the car, we stopped abruptly and looked at each other. We realized that our baby girl, Angie, was asleep in her crib upstairs. Because she was so quiet, we forgot that there was now another person, a totally dependent person, living under our roof. The reality of taking care of this baby twenty-four hours a day was suddenly upon us. Having a baby wasn't like having an automobile that we could simply park in the garage, turn the engine off, and walk away from for an hour, a day, a week, a month, or a year. We had to be completely aware, available, and responsible twenty-four hours a day. Having children is a permanent responsibility that a parent cannot just walk away from.

Most families have now become two-income families. In fact, it is rare to have it any other way these days. Because of this, the logistics become much more difficult for parents, who are trying to maintain their jobs and still raise their children with the level of care they deem necessary and desirable. And so, the logistics of having children puts even more stress on the family and on the marriage than ever before.

The stresses go still deeper. As the children grow and mature, different situations trigger memories in the parents of their own early childhood. Memories of difficulties, problems, and experiences erupt in the parents reminding them of unresolved issues that created stress on their own young minds. Often, when these memories are triggered, whether they are conscious or unconscious, frustrations and intense feelings arise for the parents, which can then cause them to dump toxic habits and hang-ups on their children.

No one is perfect. We all deal with difficult habits, thoughts, and stresses every day of our lives. How we deal with these determines our ultimate health.

Start by taking a piece of paper or a journal and write out your negative habits and behavior. What is bothering you today? This is an exercise that should be done on a regular basis. Sometimes this will be easier than others. These feelings may be about your family, work, friends, habits, any aspect of your life. Be honest with yourself. Don't be afraid to write a confession of a sin. By writing, we are not only examining and learning about ourselves. We are also bringing the thoughts and words into the hands of Jesus, who can erase any and all sin. Make a fearless moral inventory of your life.

Step 5: Share Your Inventory with Another Person

Find someone you trust spiritually and morally and share your personal inventory. This is difficult, but becomes easier as you grow in the awareness of God's love. The Bible instructs us, "Confess your sins to each other and pray for each other so that you may be healed" (James 5:16).

Remember that these are difficult steps, but they will bring you great rewards. By learning to dump these hang-ups into the hands of God, trusting him and those he sends your way, you will experience the greatest joy and peace.

Having taken these steps, you may feel exhilaration in your success. Do not stop here. This is a point where many people feel they need not go on, but this is only the fifth step out of twelve. Only if you work through the remaining steps will you discover all the beauty that God wants to give you.

Step 6: Grow Spiritually in the Lord

Recently, my wife, Donna, and I were discussing how we pray. Donna said to me, "Robert, I learned something from you about prayer."

I was surprised. I asked, "What did you learn?"

She answered, "You've taught me to always begin a prayer with thanksgiving."

I thought about it and realized for the first time that I do begin each prayer with a "thank you." I learned this from my parents. As a young boy, I accompanied my father on his hospital calls. I recall him saying to me, "When you visit someone in the hospital, Robert, always think of something the patient can be thankful for." To this day, I remember his advice.

"Thank you, Lord, for the doctors who are able to perform surgeries. Thank you, Lord, for hospitals." I mentally create a list of all the things that we can be thankful for, even though a person may be dying of cancer or experiencing high levels of pain. There is always something for which you can be thankful. As Donna and I discussed our prayer time, we decided that it was a very important ingredient to teach our children. So today our children begin their prayers with "Thank you, Jesus."

Here is a prayer that can help you get started in your new thanksgiving attitude. Use it in the morning before starting your day:

Dear God, thank you for my yesterdays, for all of them. Not just for one of them, but for all of them. Thank you, Lord, for that yesterday of pain. Thank you, Lord, for that tough time, for that difficult time. Thank you, Lord, for that time I had troubles with my parents, for the time I had trouble with my children, for everything! Lord, I now know that my yesterdays make me who I am today. God, thank you for the good times, thank you for the bad times, thank you for the rough times, thank you for the smooth times. Thank you for being there through all of it, even if I did not realize it.

After praying the prayer of thanksgiving for your yesterdays, pray a prayer of thanksgiving for today. Tomorrow may never come, and so we need to embrace today with hope and with thanks. Make the most of today because tomorrow is a gift that may never be given. We live only in the present. Don't live in your yesterdays and don't live in tomorrow. "Thank you, God, for today."

You are now ready to move into other forms of prayer. Open yourself up to God. Talk to God as if he were your very best friend. In truth, he is. Haven't you discovered that the more time you spend with someone, the closer you become? Well, it is the same way with God. The more time you spend with God—in the car, in the kitchen, when you wake up in the morning, when you wake up in the night, as you work, as you play, or when reading your Bible—the closer you become.

Step 7: Ask God to Remove Your Shortcomings

In 1 John 1:9 the Bible says, "If we confess our sins, God is faithful and just to forgive us our sins and purify us from all unrighteousness." It takes a humble person to say, "God, remove my shortcomings. I don't know why you'll do this, Lord, but I'm trusting you anyway."

In the Bible, one of Israel's judges was Gideon. One day Gideon saw a group of violent nomads, called the Midianites, coming toward the Israelites. He knew that the Midianites would leave devastation in their wake. The Midianites were known to rape the women, poison wells, and scorch the earth, leaving nothing behind but destruction. When Gideon, to his horror, saw the approaching horsemen, he prayed, "O God, what are we going to do?" And God responded to Gideon, "Rise up, you mighty man of valor, and conquer the Midianites."

And Gideon said, "Who, me? Of all the tribes of Israel, mine is the least. Of all the families of my tribe, mine is the least. Of all of the children in my tribe, I am the least. And you are telling me to rise up against this might band of men?" (Judg. 6). God was calling Gideon for a purpose. And Gideon did rise up against the Midianites; he fought against their vicious attacks and destroyed them.

God knows the enemy that threatens you today. He who called Gideon calls you to rise up and conquer your toxic habits.

Through the next two steps we will see the responsibility we need to take as individuals. The principles we have looked at rely heavily on God's sovereignty. We will now look at how important it is for our free will to align with God's. Christianity is not simply defined as a belief in the sovereignty of God, but also in our free will or response to Almighty God.

I once heard Bob Hope share the following story. It illustrates, quite well, the ageless dilemma of God's versus human will. A man answered a knock on the door of his house only to find the local sheriff with a worried look. The sheriff explained, "Sir, you have to leave your home. The flood has broken through the river levee and your house will soon be immersed in water. You must leave immediately." But the man responded, "No, I have faith in God. God will protect me."

The man stayed in his home. The water outside the man's home soon began to rise significantly. The man was up to his knees in water. The water continued to rise and was a definite threat to the man's life. Recognizing this man's plight, another man came to his aid in a boat. The skipper of the boat cried out, "Sir, climb into my boat. Hurry!" But the man replied, "No. It's all right. God's going to save me." Despite the boatman's pleas, the homeowner refused help. The boat went away.

The water continued to rise and the man was forced to climb onto his roof. The man sat there stranded, waiting for God to save him. Finally, a helicopter came and lowered a ladder. The pilot called, "Sir, grab hold of the ladder, and we'll save you!" But the man responded, "No. It's all right. God will save me." He waved the helicopter on.

The waters continued to rise until they consumed the man. He drowned. He found himself in heaven, standing before God. Confused and feeling let down, he queried, "God, why did you let me drown? Why didn't you save me?" And God answered, "I sent the sheriff. I sent a boat. I sent a helicopter. What more did you want?"

Many people find themselves in the same dilemma. How does the sovereignty of God work in relation to our own free will? The twelve steps put this dilemma into the proper perspective by positioning God first, then people second. This allows the power of God to mend and allows us to respond by taking the necessary steps to continue our course of healing toward wholeness and health.

Several years ago I watched the movie *Peter Pan* with my younger children. For those of you who know the story, what brought Peter into Wendy's bedroom? He was looking for his shadow! Peter's shadow darts through the window and into the room. Peter chases after it, and around and around the room the shadow dodges its master. Peter jumps to grab it, but the shadow escapes. The little game of tag continues until finally Peter grabs it by the heel and wrestles it to the floor of the bedroom. Wendy comes to Peter's aid and sews the shadow back on to Peter's feet so that it can't escape again.

Our shortcomings are similar to Peter's shadow. They are on the loose, and we're trying to chase them down, so that they won't embarrass us or cause others or us any trouble. Through the first seven steps we have learned how to handle our shadows. Instead of running away from the shadows of our yesterdays and hiding our pasts, we have been learning how to admit to others that our shadows do belong to us and that they are our responsibility. We have learned how to say, "This is me, folks. I've made mistakes. Here I am with all of my failures and all of my shortcomings."

Now we are on the track to becoming whole. We begin to repair some of the damage that has taken place in our lives. We have learned to face our shadows. It is time to deal with some of the problems and circumstances that are adversely affecting our relationships. Now we will look at Steps 8 and 9.

Step 8: List All Individuals You Have Harmed and Be Willing to Make Amends

This is such a difficult thing to do, because we do not want to recall those hurtful occasions: the ex-spouse whose trust we violated; the father we broke with; the mother we were harsh with; the brother or sister we abused; the grandmother or grandfather we took advantage of; the friend we betrayed.

You may have very painful memories, but you cannot skip over this step! Even memories that may not seem very significant—a child at school we stole from; the fellow employee we accused falsely; a friend we insulted. There are people you have harmed.

It's important to be honest with yourself and with God. If not, the ghosts in your memory will haunt you at the very core of your being, forcing you back into the very things that caused your shortcomings in the first place.

I had a very dear friend of mine, a senior gentleman, who was a member of a prominent family here in southern California. He was my encourager; often he would call me telling me how much he enjoyed my messages. Many times I knew a message wasn't good, but he always said it was. He was a joy to talk to.

This friend was blind, and we were working together on a project for the Braille Institute. Before the project was completed, he died, and since I knew his son well, I asked him about the funeral plans. I was informed that the family had decided not to have a funeral, just a private memorial service. I was really heartbroken. I wanted to say goodbye to my friend. I wanted the opportunity to cry and express my feelings of loss. My grief became anger. I was angry with the son for not allowing me the privilege of mourning the loss of my friend. Weeks passed and I would see the son from time to time, but I would never greet him. I would never acknowledge him. I found myself waking up at night with bad feelings.

Have you ever had something like that gnawing away at you? A relationship that forces you to walk on the other side of the street because you don't want to face a certain person? Instead of dealing with the problem, we just avoid it and let it fester inside. We think that we can ignore it, but it becomes like a hidden cancer. It will spread and infect all areas of life if we let it go too long.

There comes a point when we must be willing to look at it and then make amends. We begin by making a list, then developing a willing heart. How? Do you remember the first step? Step 1: Recognize That You Are Powerless. You don't have the power to do it, but God does. Step 2: Recognize God's Power, Look to God. And we need the grace of God to learn to love others. That doesn't mean that we become doormats. Sometimes, love means that we need to confront. But even confronting is different from harboring. When we talk out conflict, we thwart the process of hatred and bitterness. Even Jesus confronted people, but his motive was love and his goal was peace. Jesus said, "Love one another as I have loved you" (John 15:12). What power in those words! Through them come hope and healing and peace and goodness.

When you make a list of those you have harmed, list as the very first person someone each of us knows. It is someone each of us has harmed at one time or another. That someone is ourself.

Start your list by writing your name at the top, and then write what you have done or are doing that is harmful to yourself. Then it's time to make amends. You say, "How do I forgive myself for all of the tragedies I've brought to my family, to my relationships?" Look to God. As you continue to look to God, your heart will turn toward what is right. Ask God to reveal to you how much he loves you. And as you begin to see his affection toward you and draw nearer to him, you will become like him. You can learn to love, even yourself.

Now, continue with your list by writing down the names of others you have harmed and to whom you need to make amends.

Step 9: Make Amends to People You Have Harmed

Looking back to the anger I experienced over the death of my friend, I knew I had to make amends. I woke up in the middle of the night, around 2:00 A.M., and sat down to write the son a letter. I wrote, "Dear John, I have a problem and I want to tell you about it. I need to ask you for your forgiveness. I apologize for not expressing my sympathy to you, for not ministering to your needs and for the grief that you must have felt." I continued to explain my feelings and then I expressed my love for him. Do you know what? I haven't lost another night of sleep since. It brought a tremendous sense of healing and wholeness.

Write a letter to make amends, sit down face-to-face, or telephone. It doesn't matter how you do it, just make amends. Create wholeness again in broken relationships. Even if the person you have harmed refuses you, you have done what you should do and are now free from your own hatred. You will find tremendous peace. But it's up to you to take responsibility for past actions. Here's a saying I heard a long time ago that really guides me:

> Our walk talks and our talk walks,
> But our walk talks more than our talk walks.

We can talk about doing the twelve steps and know all of the right things to say, but it's another thing to actually do them. Begin today to make your list of amends and pray to God over each one. See tremendous life-changing power come your way, transforming your entire emotional state to joy and peace. Everyone will be better off because you decided to dump your hang-ups without dumping them on others.

When my younger son, Anthony, was in kindergarten, I had the privilege of attending an open house at his school. Anthony had just completed his first year in kindergarten and had learned so much. The teacher gave each parent a journal of growth made by the child in class. On the front were the words "This is Anthony Schuller on my first day of kindergarten." Below the words was an empty space for Anthony to draw a picture of himself. But it was blank. There was absolutely nothing there.

At first, I chuckled. Then, as I studied it, I thought to myself, "How many people feel just like that—that they are worth nothing in this world." If today you were assigned to draw a picture of yourself, would the page also be blank? Maybe your life is a mess. Do you feel worthless? You may know someone who does. Many people, some of whom you wouldn't suspect, feel just that way.

I told you what was on the front page of my son's kindergarten journal, but now let me tell you what was on the last page. The first page measured where he was on the first day of school. The last page measured his growth up until his last day in kindergarten. There his picture was—a collage of different shapes he'd learned to make: a circle for the head, a rectangle for the body, triangles for his feet, ovals for his ears, and a square for a hat. It took him nine months to learn how to draw these shapes and put them together. Above his head were flying birds and a shining sun and a rainbow—the promise of hope. Beneath the picture were these words: "This is Anthony Schuller in May 1993, on my last day of kindergarten."

I looked at that and thought, "This is what the twelve steps are all about—taking us from one point in our lives and transporting us to another. We can look back and see the difference. We can love ourselves."

God gives each of us the opportunity to experience spiritual growth. I believe that this can happen through the twelve steps. They are the means with which we can grow into the people God intended us to be. That doesn't mean that we suddenly arrive at a destination and we say, "Okay, I've arrived. I've made it. I have achieved it all." By no means. Life just isn't that simple. It would have been silly for my kindergartner son to end his education at that point. Life is a journey, a step-by-step, day-by-day process. Gandhi said it this way: "There's more to life than just going faster."

Step 10: Continue to Take Personal Inventory and When You Are Wrong, Promptly Admit It

Now we will go on to the last three steps. I call these the maintenance steps, because they help us to continue growing as individuals and as families. We must all practice the following principles every day. Step 10 tells us to periodically take a personal inventory of where we are in our recovery. Take an inventory of your relationships with others and with God, and, when necessary, make amends.

Before I saw the journal of growth that my son completed in kindergarten, I would not have been able to point out to you any progress that he'd made during that year. That doesn't mean that he didn't make any; it means that I had failed to keep inventory. Once I saw his journal of growth from kindergarten, the inventory that he had made, I saw the improvements.

You may be making significant progress, but if you don't take inventory, you will never know it. I would encourage you to get a journal of your own. All you need is a little blank book, or a pad of paper—anything that can be set aside for the inventory of how you are doing. Write what you do every day, what was different today from yesterday, and what you want to be different tomorrow. Just start writing. Write about how you feel. It doesn't take long to write a paragraph or two. If you feel on a certain day that you are making no improvement and are discouraged, go back and read what you wrote a month or two ago. More likely than not, you will see a difference.

Step 11: Pray for God's Will to Be Done in Your Life

This is a difficult step. We recognize that we are surrendering all we are and have to the will of a higher power—God. This happens only through prayer and meditation. You must come with a prayerful heart saying, "God, open my mind to your way and to your will."

A story is told about a man who was dying in the hospital. His temperature was running high and there wasn't much hope for him. It was believed that he might not make it through the night. The dying man could barely make out that he happened to be sharing a room. The roommate was naturally very concerned for this extremely sick and dying man. He saw the man looking chalky white. He heard him having convulsions and he felt terrible for the man. He began praying for him in his heart. Forgetting all about his own condition, the roommate prayed for some time until he fell asleep.

When he awoke the following morning, the praying man felt much better than he had in days. His own fever had broken, and his vital signs were stabilized. His condition was dramatically improved. For the first time in days, he sat up and ate. He then noticed that the bed next to him was empty. Concern turned his stomach. He turned to the nurse and asked, "Please, tell me, what happened to the man in the bed next to mine?"

The nurse replied, "There was never a man in the bed next to you."

He said, "What do you mean? I know there was a man in that bed. I saw him there last night. He was very sick. Please, if he has died, I want to know."

The nurse was puzzled. After discussing the odd conversation with some other nurses, they figured out that the man, in a delirious state the night before, must have looked into the window and seen his own reflection. The compassion he felt the night before for an ill stranger had turned into prayers for himself. And thus the healing came.

We find that God's will is for us to look beyond ourselves to others who are hurting and reach out to touch them. That leads us to the next step.

Step 12: Reach Out and Touch Others in
a Positive and Inspiring Way

The last step has now arrived. This is where the circle becomes complete. Having had a spiritual awakening as a result of walking through the twelve steps, we, in turn, carry the message to others. As we practice all twelve steps in our everyday activities, we bless others and help those who are struggling with addictions and negative habits who want to begin the walk and find the salvation they need.

Once you have walked the path, you are now able to support others who are just starting on their journey. This will be both frustrating and rewarding. Although it is painful to see others fall, it is rewarding to see them overcome the temptations. The best part of all will be watching your own growth as you continue down this path of detoxification. I am sure you have heard it said, "The best way to learn something is to teach it." In Step 12 you become the teacher in spiritual enlightenment.

Possibility Living involves keeping these twelve steps before you. Review them each day. You can enjoy life and those around you. Don't neglect yourself or others any longer. Dump your toxic habits and hang-ups and you will discover what life is all about—love, peace, and joy with those around you and with the One who created you. Do it now!

CHAPTER 12

DETOXIFY YOUR PHYSIOLOGY

Dr. Douglas Di Siena

God did not direct the creation of our bodies for forty weeks just to leave us masterless as we enter the world. He gave us an inborn intelligence, a wisdom that resides in us all. The apostle John wrote, "The Spirit who lives in you is greater than the spirit who lives in the world" (1 John 4:4, NLT). This Spirit of wisdom, which monitors, repairs, organizes, and ultimately resurrects our entire body cell by cell, flows via the nervous system. When this intelligence flows, a wonderful cellular dance of life occurs. The body is functioning optimally and is in harmony with both itself and the world. However, stress, autointoxication, and trauma can all result in blocking the expression of this innate, God-given intelligence. This process results in a dis-eased body. A dis-eased body loses the ability to constructively respond to an ever changing environment. Less able to eliminate toxins, monitor foreign invaders, e.g., cancer cells, viruses, and bacteria, the body slows down the repairing process, which results in aging, and ultimately loses its ability to maintain an organized state, causing organ systems to become dysfunctional, leading to disabilities, decay, and an early death. We call this "toxic physiology."

Dr. Bernie Siegel wrote, "It follows that whatever upsets the brain's control of the immune system will foster malignancy."[1] I believe that the most neglected part of our body with respect to heath and wellness is the mind/nervous system. No other organ has so much power to heal and to cause disease. It has been said that life itself is a manifestation of the Spirit expressing itself in the mind/nervous system. Recently, there has been considerable information relating our thoughts to their effect on our health. In this chapter, we want to reveal the keys to keeping our nervous system fully functional.

I attended a meeting with Dr. William Kellas, an expert on toxicity whom I respect and admire. We experience two completely different professional worlds, yet we share many of the same goals, passions, and philosophies. Recently, we were exchanging ideas on the causes of toxicity. He believes that toxicity is at the root of many diseases. He went on to say that the two most frequent and dangerous causes of toxicity were toxic dental work and spinal trauma. Most people are not aware that spinal trauma has a significant detrimental impact on our health and wellness.

1. *Toxic dental work.* The issue of toxic dental work should be of great concern. I have many dentists as patients in my office who no longer put in amalgam fillings. Amalgam contains mercury, a well-known toxin.

2. *Spinal trauma.* Trauma to spine, e.g., whiplash, results in subluxation (nerve irritation due to spinal dysfunction). Although whiplash obviously can cause subluxation, many times the most severe cause of neck injury results from birth trauma. Many studies, some of which we will reference in this chapter, discuss the cervical trauma from the typical American childbirth process.

As Dr. Kellas uttered that statement, I couldn't help but stand up and cheer in my joy of being affirmed from someone I so respect. D. D. Palmer, the founder of chiropractic, stated back in 1910, "The determining causes of disease are traumatism, poison, and auto-suggestion." Dr. Kellas was echoing Dr. Palmer's idea of the *Above, Down, Inside,*

Out principle and the cause of disease.[2] I will simply put Dr. Palmer's principle into more modern terminology. The three toxic stressors that inhibit the body from optimally functioning and responding to its environment are these:

1. trauma (subluxation, causing toxicity)

2. poison (toxicity)

3. autosuggestion, or toxic/negative thoughts

I have continued to devote my professional life to studying these principles. Through my research, I can conclude that these principles hold true. The idea of the mind-body connection is now a cultural hot topic. Any trip to the local bookstore proves the immense popularity of the subject. Many authors are writing about it, yet there is little understanding from a practical, physical point of view. How do we take what we know about this connection and make it work from day to day? The truth is that it is possible for everyone to maintain optimal function of your mind-body connection.

THE POWER THAT CREATED THE BODY HEALS THE BODY

It was New Year's Eve 1995. We had some family over, and my then five-year-old daughter, Alex, who typically loves all of the attention, was mysteriously absent from the party. I went into the family room and found her on the couch. She said she was not feeling well and asked if I could hold her for a while. As she was in my arms, I reminded her how much junk food she had been eating and asked her to promise me that tomorrow she would throw away the rest of the chocolate and fudge she received as presents. After she fell to sleep, I rejoined the party thinking that Alex probably just ate too much junk food during the holiday week.

As I was getting into bed that night, my wife heard Alex asking for one of us to come into her room. We found her to be very pale, feverish, and nauseous. Evidently, every time she tried to get up to go to the bathroom she was too dizzy. She told us her ear was hurting. I adjusted her that night and put her to bed. The next day she was somewhat better; however, that next night would prove to be a faith test for all of us. Shortly after we all went to bed, we again heard Alex calling for us. My wife went to see her and within minutes my wife was frantically calling for me. As I walked into Alex's room, my wife pointed to her ear flaring out 90 degrees from her head. I feared she could have a rare condition called mastoiditis.

I had read many pediatric texts over the years, but remembered one pediatric expert in particular. Dr. Mendelsohn said that while mastoiditis can occur, he had never seen it in his private practice, and it was a very rare occurrence. In a panic, I ran back into my office and looked it up in all of my pediatric books, hoping this wasn't mastoiditis. However, to my to my disbelief, it was mastoiditis, or osteomyelitis of the mastoid bone, a potentially very serious disease. Although very rare, an ear infection can spread into the adjacent mastoid bone just behind the ear. As the infection moves into the bone, it fills up with puss and blows the bone up like a balloon; this causes incredible pain in and around the ear. By this time, my wife had brought her to our room, where I adjusted her again and proceeded to pray.

I told my wife that the next morning we would have to take her in for a medical evaluation and that the only course of treatment they had for this condition was to cut into the eardrum for drainage. If that didn't help, they would surgically remove the mastoid part of the skull, leaving her permanently disfigured. She then would be hospitalized and given massive amounts of intravenous antibiotics to prevent the spread of infection.

The rest of that night we rhythmically prayed, and I adjusted her. We repeated this hour after hour until I was so exhausted I literally collapsed with the adjusting instrument still in my hand. I was not only grieving for my daughter's pain and suffering; I was also intensely questioning my judgment, ability, and the A.D.I.O. principle. I was very successful in my practice, and not one of the kids under my care ever got this sick. Yet I couldn't adequately take care of my own child, my firstborn, my special "sweetness." If I couldn't help her, I only wished I could take on all her pain.

It must have been only a couple of hours since the last time I adjusted and prayed over her, but when we woke, to our amazement, there was no longer a lump behind her ear. Alex's ear laid back perfectly against her skull as before. Her fever was down, and color had returned to her face. The restoration of her ear could only have occurred by the supernatural. It was a miracle. That night we cried out for help, and God's presence healed my baby. All through the preceding days, we prayed without ceasing. We also took responsibility to do everything we were called to do to remove any blockage and allow the body to receive the healing power of God.

God called me to be a chiropractor and to live and spread the A.D.I.O. message. I believe he tested us in our faith and in the A.D.I.O. principle. I also believe that this both strengthened my resolve and equipped me for his service in the healing ministry. I learned he is in control, and I am only a servant, a laborer who must be committed to his work. Only he deserves the credit and the praise for all healing, whether it is from a small scrape or cancer.

God made no mistakes in making our body. The definition of a healthy body is one in which all of the parts are functioning at optimal levels. The nervous system is the mechanism that monitors the functioning of the body. Additionally, the nervous system seems to transmit intelligent power, which animates or gives life properties to every tissue in the body. This intelligence gives order to the system and allows for the proper response to the environment—the key to keeping us well.

We were created as a functional and structural whole. I am often asked in my practice if we really need our appendix, and I prefer to answer the question with a more philosophical approach. I maintain that God did not make us with unnecessary parts. If we have an appendix, we need it. When I was growing up in the 1960s, a routine surgery was removing the tonsils. Fortunately, we now know that the tonsils are also a lymphoid tissue and have a very important job in fighting off disease. Keep this equation in mind:

Innate Intelligence = Ability to Respond to the Environment = Health

As we have stated before, when the body loses its ability to respond to the environment it begins a decaying (toxic) process. For instance, if I were to tear the leather seat in my car, I would have to get the leather repaired. If, however, I were to tear a piece of skin off my hand, my hand would make hundreds of thousands of modifications at the cellular level to first stop the bleeding, then ultimately replace the skin. Let us say I continue to scratch my hand; the body would respond by replacing the normal skin with a more resilient scar tissue we call a callus. Our body, which is made up of matter, is designed to be an expression of this intelligence. The chiropractic profession calls this "innate intelligence." The difference between the inanimate leather and the skin on my hand is that my skin is expressing innate intelligence.

Our bodies were developed and designed by God (Gen. 1–2; Ps. 139). Is it likely that this same God, after knitting us together in our mother's womb, would leave us disorganized and susceptible to any outside force without an internal intelligence waiting to be called upon to rebuild and reorganize at times of stress? Of course not. Without innate intelligence, we would literally fall apart.

It is interesting to know that our bodies are really nothing but space. Just how much space? Well, our bodies are made up of atoms. Imagine, if you will, the nucleus of one atom blown up to the size of a honeydew melon; the electron (part of the atom that spins around the nucleus) would be the equivalent to three thousand miles away. At the subatomic level, our bodies are really nothing but a vast amount of space. Furthermore, in the nucleus of the atom are protons, subatomic particles with a positive charge. Anyone who has ever played with a magnet knows that like charges repel. What keeps our atoms from exploding? Scientists know it must be an extremely powerful force or energy. For a lack of a better term, they call this energy "atomic glue." In fact, the atomic bomb gets its explosive force by breaking the bond of the "atomic glue."

That which holds all things together and keeps all matter organized

I call innate intelligence. This is God's creative power in us. Paul writes about it this way:

> Christ is the visible image of the invisible God. He existed before God made anything at all and is supreme over all creation. Christ is the one through whom God created everything in heaven and earth. He made the things we can see and the things we can't see—kings, kingdoms, rulers, and authorities. Everything has been created through him and for him. He existed before everything else began, and he holds all creation together."
>
> Colossians 1:15–17

"Greater is he that is in me than he that is in the world" (1 John 4:4). The "he" that the Scriptures are referring to is God's Spirit, who is the "innate intelligence" and the "atomic glue" holding us together. His power utilizes the nervous system as a communication network, flooding the entire body with this powerful healing intelligence.

Dr. Albert Schweitzer said, "Each patient carries his own doctor inside him. They come to us not knowing that truth. We are at our best when we give the Doctor which resides within each patient a chance to go to work." He is talking about the Great Physician. God gave us all the gift of the Great Physician. All we need to do is remove any blockages that might prevent his power of healing and regeneration from working.

Often when describing the nervous system and its role in healing and health, I like to compare it to a classical music conductor. When we hear just the right individual notes coming from a variety of musical instruments combined at the right tempo, it sounds glorious. This is because a conductor monitors, directs, and controls the individual musicians. When the sounds get to our ears we hear harmonious, beautiful music. Your nervous system works in a similar fashion.

To get an idea of the details and precision of the nervous system, consider that the number of cells in the human body is estimated at 50 billion. Each one of those cells has a multitude of responsibilities. Let us take the liver cell; at the latest count, its number of functions is over five hundred. With a little multiplication one can begin to imagine how miraculously designed we are. Yet with so many cellular functions going on at all times, it is no wonder that, as Dr. Bernie Siegel states, "It follows that whatever upsets the brain's control of the immune system will foster malignancy."

Whatever upsets the brain's control over any organ system will bring disease to the system. Going back to the orchestra, if for some reason the conductor suffers a sudden deafening ringing in the ears, the feedback loop would be broken. If the conductor cannot hear the music, he can no longer facilitate a harmonious balance of all the sounds. It is the same with our body. If the feedback mechanism is broken in any way, the brain loses its capacity to facilitate a harmonious balance of all the countless cellular processes going on at any given moment. "The nervous system is the mechanism concerned with the correlation and integration of various bodily processes, the reactions and adjustments of the organism to its environment."[3] The pioneer chiropractors have long believed that the source of disease results from the body being unable to respond to its environment. For the purposes of illustration, let's assume that a well person consumed food that was slightly ill prepared and therefore had some toxic bacteria. As the food enters the intestine, there begins this most incredible series of events. The body senses the toxin, and signals to the brain. The brain processes the information, and then responds. It signals back to the various organs. The organs immediately and precisely eliminate or contain all of the toxins. This is like a beautifully orchestrated piece of music with the conductor monitoring every sound, and directing the concerto. Each musician plays their particular instrument in perfect harmony. All of this physiological response occurs many more times then we could even appreciate, and most of the time we are not even slightly aware that our body has just saved us from disease.

We might ask why, if the innate intelligence is so smart, we ever get sick at all. The answer to that question is obstruction. Anytime this intelligence is inhibited from its fullest expression, we are dimming the expression of life, and thus we become more susceptible to disease. Let's explore some reasons our physiology becomes toxic.

The mind-body connection. In 1974 Robert Ader, a psychologist at the University of Rochester, did a brilliant study discovering for the first time the role of the mind in relation to the immune system. First he conditioned a group of rats to associate nausea with sugar water by injecting them with a nausea-producing drug just before giving them sugar water. This is similar to the conditioning that Pavlov did when he got his dogs to salivate at the sound of a bell. Ader then continued his study by stopping the drug and waiting to see just how long it would take the rats to forget their "nausea conditioning" to the sugar water. Interestingly, on the forty-fifth day, some of the rats began to die for seemingly unknown reasons. All of the rats were well fed and kept in good condition, and thus he was puzzled why some were dying. Upon further study, he found that the rats that were dying were the ones who were drinking the most sugar water.

Ader's amazing discovery was that rats were not dying due to the sugar water itself, but from what they believed about the sugar water. The cornerstone to his discovery was what he had used to create the nausea conditioning in the rats. To create the nausea, Ader used cyclophosphamid, more commonly called Cytoxan, a drug routinely used for chemotherapy. Cytoxan happens to be a strong immunosuppressant (it suppresses the immune system). Ader's conclusion was that it was the nausea conditioning to the sugar water that actually killed the rats. Even though the actual drug had been out of their systems for quite a while, every time the rats consumed the sugar water they associated it with the immunosuppressant effect of Cytoxan. With each drink of the plain sugar water, the rats believed they were getting more Cytoxan. Their immune systems were decreasing in ability to function, thus leaving the rats more susceptible to disease. Ader continued to do exhaustive research. In 1981, he concluded that the immune system did not function independently, but was controlled by the mind and the nervous system. He entitled his book *Psychoneuroimmunology.* This was a new name for the functioning of the mind-body connection and the role it plays in our health.[4]

DETOXING THOUGHTS WORKS TO DETOX THE BODY

Earlier in this book we discussed how detoxifying our thoughts helps our bodies be less stressed and subject to disease. If negative, stressful thoughts can bring about a breakdown in the mechanism controlling the body, then thinking good thoughts, thoughts of love, joy, peace, patience, and kindness can bring about healing. We have reiterated the importance of the proper connection of the mind to the body and how stress can be a blockage to the free flow of our innate intelligence, resulting in a toxic state in the body. We need to now understand how this connection or communication of the mind and body occurs. As Dr. Ader has "rediscovered," the nervous system is the communication system that connects the mind and body.

SUBLUXATIONS CAUSE TOXIC PHYSIOLOGY

If the communication network between mind and body were to fail, what would happen to the system? Like any other relationship, from marriage to top-level international diplomacy, the lines of communication must be open. The skull and twenty-four movable vertebrae surround the central nervous system. One of the functions of these vertebrae is to act as a shield of armor to protect the nervous system. Unfortunately, these same protective vertebrae can misalign, become dysfunctional, and develop into a condition called subluxation. Researchers have revealed that subluxation reduce the ability of the nerve to function.[5] Subluxation is detrimental to our health and well-being. Subluxations cause nerve interference, resulting in an altered bodily expression and a decrease in the ability to function optimally.

AUTOINTOXICATION CAUSES TOXIC PHYSIOLOGY

One of the most common ways we begin to enter a toxic state is through a process we call autointoxication. This process occurs when we alter the innate intelligence. For example, if we lose normal alignment in our neck, which can happen as early as birth, the resulting brain-stem pressure compresses and/or irritates the nerves. One nerve often affected in this way is the vagus nerve (derived from the Latin word for "wandering"). This nerve extends to most of our regulatory and digestive organs. So if you were to lose optimal function in this nerve alone, your body would no longer digest food or eliminate waste and thus would become very toxic (autointoxication).

Spinal subluxations are real, often occurring at birth.[6] They can cause dysfunction and toxicity, but can be corrected gently and safely only by a qualified chiropractor. Birth-related injuries to the spine are mostly underreported. One only has to watch the birth process to see how much stress is applied to the cervical spine. The spine of a newborn can typically be pulled with up to fifty pounds of traction force. If that is not enough to cause soft-tissue trauma, as soon as the head is delivered, it is then twisted almost 90 degrees. This action forces the shoulders to twist, allowing for the rest of the body to be delivered as quickly as possibly. To get a perspective on this experience, think of holding up a one-day-old infant with little muscle tone, since he or she has been floating in fluid for nine months, solely by the head.

Add five bowling balls to the infant's feet, all the while twisting the neck so that the chin is next to the shoulder. That is how much strain the little neck must endure coming into this world. Combine that trauma with all of those falls the baby begins to accumulate in the quest to walk. Now add bike, skateboard, and sports injuries, let alone the many other causes of chronic toxic subluxation patterns, which will persist unless corrected.

In our office, we always include the children when both spouses are under care. Children always need to be checked for subluxations because they do not have the ability to communicate, and even if they did, it may not help since subluxation does not always cause symptoms. We passionately feel that children can never grow to their full potential with a life-restricting subluxation. We also want children to grasp the A.D.I.O. paradigm. If children are brought in for wellness care or even for a particular condition, it is not too long before they realize that we look first to the power from *above* to supply all of our needs. If the children become ill, whether physically or emotionally, they will not have the ingrained reflex to seek a drug, but rather to first seek relief from *above*.

There is a necessary ingredient for our ability to express wellness. That ingredient is the power, or intelligence, that comes from *above* and utilizes the mind-body connection. This intelligence/power flows via the nervous system. For us to be as healthy as we want to be, we need to remove any possible stress from the nervous system and allow for the power to manifest itself in every tissue and cell in our body. The A.D.I.O. principle leads to the abundant life through Possibility Living.

Chiropractic is an art and science ahead of its time. One hundred years ago when chiropractic began to establish the role the nervous system plays in health and in the cause of dis-ease, the established medical community's focus was on treating the diseased blood; hence the practice of bleeding was very much accepted as a "scientific" approach to treating illnesses. In addition to bleeding, the medical establishment believed in poisoning what remaining blood was left in the patient with such toxic substances as arsenic, strychnine, and mercurials.[7] Additionally, patients with infected skin lesions had their flesh burned, not only causing tremendous amounts of pain, but severe disfigurement as well. These treatments were oftentimes, if not mostly, worse than the patients' original complaints.

At the time when D. D. Palmer began to teach a new principle (a principle that recognizes the nervous system as the master controller of the body, and that when there is pressure on a nerve, the nerve is unable to transmit impulses from the brain, ultimately creating an organism susceptible to disease), he was scoffed at by the medical establishment. After all, the paradigm at the time was to treat the blood; that's where the germs were. The idea that health comes from *Above, Down, Inside, Out* was radical, if not heretical. Fortunately, this type of approach caught on like wildfire. Remember the alternative. Not only was chiropractic proving itself with results; the care offered by the chiropractor was safe, painless, and inexpensive. So who is surprised that, over one hundred years later, notable doctors in the medical profession as well as the research communities are propagating the chiropractic principle.

A.D.I.O. LEADS TO TOXIN-FREE PHYSIOLOGY

When do you want to start living a life free from the physical effects of emotional stress, free from the toxins resulting from subluxation, nerve pressure, and dysfunction, free from the separation of the physical and spiritual?

The A.D.I.O. principle is about getting connected to the Source. It is the immutable truth that will always set you free. God *above* has come *down* and created your body to contain his innate wisdom and intelligence. From *inside* flows *out* his health and love.

CHAPTER 13

DETOXIFY YOUR RELIGION

Dr. Robert A. Schuller

The term "spiritual abuse" was coined in the late 1980s with the rise of the "Christian" twelve-step movement. When the twelve steps for Alcoholics Anonymous (AA) were developed, they were intended by Christian men to reach the alcoholic who did not have enough self-confidence to believe God existed, let alone believe in God's love for him. Since the twelve-step movement began nearly a hundred years ago, it has spread to reach all kinds of addictions.

One of the things we barely touched on earlier in our discussion of detoxing habits is the issue of spiritual abuse. Many religious habits and beliefs can become toxic. Toxic religious habits and beliefs are not confined to a specific denomination or geographical region. They are sprinkled throughout society in every corner and home across America and around the world.

Spiritual abuse is the dangerous side of religion. Religious belief has the immense power to motivate and shape lives. As a result, it has been used by a variety of leaders with various motivations to manipulate people for certain gains. This has been happening from the beginning of time. No religion is free from this manipulation.

TOXIC RELIGION BEGAN WITH
ANCIENT RELIGIOUS MANIPULATION

The ancient Greeks were the first to recognize the role of religion in politics. As their empire expanded, they incorporated the gods of the peoples they conquered into their pantheon. They didn't try to fight the local gods, because they realized that that was a battle they could not win. The Romans also adopted this religious policy. It worked for them as well, except with a small band of renegades in the east known as Hebrews. The Jewish people believed in only one God, and to add their God to that pantheon was a sacrilege. To erect any statues to other gods in their city would cause a riot. Since Rome wanted peace at all costs, the empire was resigned to making religious concessions. But there was a limit to this leniency. When the Hebrews, who were already given special dispensation, caused problems over a man called the Messiah, the reaction was swift and cruel. The Pax Romana, the "Roman peace," had to be maintained. Therefore a man was sacrificed to calm the religious zealots. It was not the first time or last time that this was done.

Crucifixion of political enemies was common. The crucifixion of one man named Jesus did not make any difference to Rome. But this time the trouble didn't end when he died. His followers didn't disappear. The problems with the Hebrews continued.

Ultimately Rome just decided to exterminate the Jews and its sect called The Way. Rome believed that by destroying the Jewish temple in Jerusalem in A.D. 72 and persecuting Christians throughout the empire, its religious and political problems would be solved. From Rome's perspective, killing off the Jews would bring political and religious peace. This wasn't the first time or the last time someone would attempt to exterminate the Jewish people. In spite of horrific persecutions by emperors like Nero and Domitian, Christianity prospered for the next three hundred years and the grip of the Roman political and religious state weakened. "Those Christians just will not succumb to the normal pressures we present," the Romans complained. "We even feed them to the lions and we still cannot control them. They just do not cooperate." The Roman Empire eventually collapsed, but what remained was a faith centered in the Messiah, Jesus.

In the Middle Ages, political and religious leaders were able to infiltrate the hierarchy of the church and manipulate its leadership. Those who would abuse slowly changed the philosophy of the church. They reasoned that if people could go to God, ask him for forgiveness, and receive the gift of grace, they would be left without the tools to manipulate and control. So they made up some conditions for salvation, something to hang over the people's heads. Holding the key to salvation through, say, "penance" for God's grace, they could get people to march into war, sell their positions, and do just about anything to avoid eternal damnation. When the ruling elite and the church hierarchy controlled the masses through spiritual manipulation, the result was a dark period for the church of Jesus Christ. During the millennium before the Reformation and the renaissance of spiritual freedom that began in the sixteenth century, spiritual abuse was rampant in the Christian landscape.

TOXIC RELIGION REPLACES GRACE WITH WORKS

Today, there are still those who wish to use Christianity for their own purposes. To do this, they remove the grace of Christ and replace it with a salvation by works. This works-based salvation is earned by doing whatever a manipulator tells the members to do. It is no wonder that Communists call religion the "opium of the masses." Without the free gift of God's love and grace, religion does become toxic and addictive. It is used to destroy self-esteem and tear down self-confidence.

Faith is a relationship, not a religion. What gave the early Christians power to overthrow governments was the fact that their belief system was not connected to politics or any form of government. The persons who responded to the Good News of Jesus Christ did not become more religious. They simply developed a relationship with a spiritual being—a relationship that could be fully understood only through experience. Once experienced, this relationship would be embraced, for no person who has ever been touched by the Holy Spirit of God is ever the same. Jesus promised that he would be sending a comforter to care for his disciples. No one knew what that meant until they experienced it.

After the ascension of Christ into heaven, the apostles and other disciples gathered in a room in Jerusalem to wait and pray. They were fearful and powerless, afraid that the Jewish law was going to take the next step in its desire to abolish this heresy and imprison or kill those closest to Jesus. Their fears were warranted.

It was during the time of the harvest festival of the Jewish people, called Pentecost. Jews from all over the world were there to celebrate this special feast. All Jews were encouraged to come to Jerusalem for the feast at least once in their lifetime. Once in Jerusalem, they would set up tents in the squares and on the flat roofs of the homes and the city would buzz with excitement.

Suddenly, a "flame of fire" bounced throughout that room and touched the apostles and disciples with the gift of speaking in foreign languages. It was a miraculous event. Without fear and with a new boldness and confidence, the apostles and disciples went out into the streets and began to share the Good News of Jesus Christ and his love. Peter delivered a sermon and that day three thousand believed in Jesus. These new believers went from Jerusalem into the entire world proclaiming the Good News that Jesus was alive. Even if the religious leaders in Jerusalem executed all of the apostles, the church would still survive.

The Jewish people who came to Jerusalem that year were there to celebrate a harvest of crops that had been reaped. Little did they know that the reason for the celebration would be the harvest of their own souls.

The Holy Spirit gave the gift of foreign language, the gift of courage, and the gift of renewed life. The account of the Acts of the Apostles in the New Testament reports how the empowering Holy Spirit transformed a band of frightened followers into a mighty army of believers. The world was turned upside down.

The Holy Spirit is the third part of the Trinity. God's Spirit imparts his favor and will upon flesh. It was in the beginning with God. We read about it in Genesis, "and the spirit of God was hovering over the face of the waters" (Gen. 1:2). God's Spirit led the Israelites through the wilderness as a pillar of fire by night and a pillar of cloud by day. David the psalmist knew of the Spirit when he prayed, "And do not take Your Holy Spirit from me" (Psalm 51:11). Centuries before Christ foretold that the comforting Spirit would come, Joel prophesied, "And it shall come to pass afterward that I will pour out My Spirit on all flesh; Your sons and your daughters shall prophesy, Your old men shall dream dreams, Your young men shall see visions. . . . And it shall come to pass that whoever calls on the name of the Lord shall be saved" (Joel 2:28–32). Clearly, the Holy Spirit has been with God from the beginning and will be with us forever more.

The Holy Spirit gives us an opportunity to have more than a religion. He creates within us a relationship through Christ with the living God. Some people in their joy of having a relationship for the first time have thrown out all their religion. The prayers they were taught, the robes that were worn, the pomp and circumstance of the religion and respectful worship. These things are not good or bad in and of themselves. They are only good or bad in the way in which they enhance or diminish your means of worship and praise. It comes down to personal preference. We need to be tolerant of different types of worship, as all kinds that come from the heart are pleasing to God.

TOXIC RELIGION JUDGES OTHERS

Toxic religion starts very innocently. It enters conversation in the subtlest ways, often asking the basic question, "What is a Christian?" followed by the statement, "Just because he goes to church doesn't mean he's a Christian."

At the turn of the last century, a holiness movement swept across America asking this question. It divided denominations. My own, The Reformed Church in America was split. The splinter group called itself the "Christian" Reformed Church in America, the implication being that the original church really wasn't Christian. Why weren't they Christians? Well, they were allowed to smoke, go to the cinema, dance, drink alcoholic beverages, use playing cards and dice, and many other things that the new church deemed "unholy." Now a hundred years later, there is no difference between the two denominations and the likelihood of a future merger is great.

Jesus said, "Judge not lest you be judged" (Matt. 7:1). This means that I must not judge others in their Christian beliefs. I must test my own faith regularly, but never someone else's. If individuals tell me they are Christians, I must believe them. I am not the judge; God is, and they will have to stand before him and be judged. As for me, I know that I am ready—not wanting to go, but ready. As the saying goes, "Everybody wants to go to heaven, but nobody wants to die."

In toxic religion, there are earthly judges who decide whether you are saved or lost. Only God can judge. God has kept this act for himself. Toxic religion tries to make people judges and remove God from that authority.

TOXIC RELIGION FOCUSES SALVATION ON PEOPLE, NOT JESUS

"I thought Jesus gave the keys of heaven to St. Peter." I hear this statement often. It refers to a passage of Scripture in which Jesus responds to Peter's profession of faith. The Roman Catholic church has used this passage to give credence to the authority of the pope, saying that the keys given to St. Peter have been passed down through the centuries to the current pope.

> Jesus asked his disciples, saying, "Who do men say that I, the Son of Man, am?"
> So they said, "Some say John the Baptist, some Elijah, and others Jeremiah or one of the prophets."
> He said to them, "But who do you say that I am?"
> And Simon Peter answered and said, "You are the Christ, the Son of the living God."

> Jesus answered and said to him, "Blessed are you, Simon Bar-Jonah, for flesh and blood has not revealed this to you, but My Father who is in heaven.
>
> "And I also say to you that you are Peter, and on this rock I will build My church and the gates of Hades shall not prevail against it.
>
> "And I will give you the keys of the kingdom of heaven, and whatever you bind on earth will be bound in heaven, and whatever you loose on earth will be loosed in heaven."
>
> Matthew 16:13–19

This is one of the most beautiful passages in the New Testament. I love the boldness with which Peter stands up and professes his knowledge of the Christ and verbally names Jesus of Nazareth the Messiah. This is the first time that any of his disciples make any such declaration. The apostles were suspicious from the beginning. After all the miracles and teaching, the implications were there, but never the pronouncement. Now the air is cleared. The speculation is over. Peter nails it, "You are the Christ, the son of the living God." Peter receives a new name, the Greek word "Petros," which means "rock." Jesus is saying, "Simon by making that statement you become as rock and upon that rock I will build my church and the gates of hell shall not prevail against it." It isn't the person that the church of Jesus Christ is built upon, but the statement from that person: "You are the Christ, the son of the living God." There is a powerful difference here.

If the church is built upon a person, then the church can fall with that person. As we see later in the New Testament, Peter, the "rock," denies Christ three times. As individuals, we all fail. The statement, however, will never fail. It is as sure as the day it was written. Whoever calls upon that statement, whoever says of Jesus "You are the Christ, the son of the living God," will be bound for heaven. The statement of the keys refers to all who recognize Jesus. Each person who individually declares that statement receives the keys for his or her future and the name "Petros." They each become rock. They each hold the key to their own destiny. This interpretation is toxin-free and empowering.

We see this truth in other biblical passages such as Jesus' statement, "No one comes to the Father except through me" (John 14:6). Talking to the twelve disciples, Jesus said, "Go into all the world and preach the gospel to every creature. He who believes and is baptized will be saved; and he who does not believe will be condemned" (Mark 16:15–16).

If the keys had been given to Peter only, why here are they dispersed to all the apostles? Let us go a step further and say that not only have the keys been given to Peter and the apostles, but a key has been given to you. Since you hold the key to your eternity, use it and enjoy it today. Don't let anyone dangle a carrot of salvation in front of you and manipulate you with it. God has already given it to you, and all you have to do is use it.

TOXIC RELIGION ASKS WHAT WOULD PEOPLE DO, INSTEAD OF WWJD?

If we are saved through grace, what is our motivation to do good? This question has been a criticism of Christianity for centuries. It is another means by which toxic thinking enters a healthy religion. Sanctification is a big "churchy" word meaning the living out of our faith. It is the process by which Christian actions grow closer to what Jesus would do. The actions of a healthy Christian model those of Jesus Christ. The question is asked, "What would Jesus do?" In fact many wear necklaces or other jewelry with the initials WWJD, which stand for "What Would Jesus Do?"

One morning two brothers were fighting over who would get the first pancake for breakfast. Finally, Mom stepped in and turned to Ryan, the older, all of eight years, and asked, "What does you bracelet say?"

"WWJD," he sighed.

"That's right, Ryan. And what does it mean?"

"What Would Jesus Do?" he sighed.

Turning to his little five-year-old brother he sparked up, "Okay, Jimmy, you be Jesus."

Possibility Living understands that our goal is not to act like Jesus in order to get into heaven. Getting into heaven has already been determined by our confession of faith in Christ. Our motivation to live like

Jesus is for personal, earthly reasons. The course of events that will bring us the greatest joy life offers is to follow the path that Jesus would follow. Following Jesus is the key to life's greatest possibilities.

DETOXIFY RELIGION WITH GRATITUDE IN ACTION

Another motivation we have for doing good is to show gratitude to God for all that he has done for us. One outline I learned in seminary was "guilt, grace, and gratitude."

Guilt: We are all guilty of sin and deserving of punishment. No one has the means alone to earn his or her way into heaven. The Old Testament is full of prophets who tried to live up to the law and earn their way, yet not one lived a perfect life. Moses was a murderer and David was an adulterer. We can go through the Old Testament and find many others to prove that no one is perfect. We are all in need of God's forgiveness.

Grace: God decided to offer us a new promise, a new covenant. Through his Son, Jesus Christ, he offers us his grace. It is a free ticket to heaven from God. Call upon the name of Jesus and you will be saved. Is that simple enough or what? The new promise won't let you earn your way into heaven. Heaven is a gift.

Trying to earn your way to heaven is like trying to swim to Hawaii. If you are like me, you might be able to swim about a mile before you start to sink. Or you may be one of he greatest swimmers in the world and have the stamina to swim a hundred miles or more. Regardless of whether you swim like me or like a marathoner, the time will come when you cannot take another stroke. Instead of sinking to the bottom, Jesus comes to you in his lifeboat and says, "I'll take you the rest of the way to Hawaii." He reaches out to you, pulls you out of the cold water, and sets you securely in the boat.

Gratitude: With a heart of gratitude for the lift to Hawaii, we simply ask him, "Is there anything I can do to help out while we make our way there?" "Yes," he says, "follow me and love one another." We start living a life of love based not on a hope of eternal life, but on gratitude for the love that was already shown for us.

SUPPORT FOR THE ABUSED

Today, there are twelve-step groups for those who have been spiritually abused. They have been very helpful in bringing people out of toxic religious experiences and into health. The key to success in breaking out of a toxic religion is found in the twelve steps outlined in Chapter 11. These same steps have worked wonders in helping those who have been lost in spiritual abuse.

You can also seek out a church where the emphasis is on loving relationships in Christ, instead of ritual and religious manipulation. If you find yourself in a religious setting that seeks to manipulate, control, dominate, or intimidate you, let the Holy Spirit lead you away from that to a faith community whose members love God and one another. Jesus said, "Your love for one another will prove to the world that you are my disciples" (John 13:35).

There is help. Peace waits on the other side. You will never know how heavy your baggage is until you set it down. If you have tried over and over again to be freed from the baggage of guilt and shame, but find yourself still carrying it around, dragging it from one relationship to another, dumping it on the people you love, you need to get in touch with the appropriate twelve-step group. It is a safe place to get started. When the time comes and you are able to find the freedom from the spiritual abuse and pain, it will be the greatest day of your life.

Possibility Living is a relationship with Jesus Christ, not a religion of works and manipulation. Possibility Living embraces God's grace and is empowered by His Spirit. Possibility Living is a life filled with gratitude and thanksgiving to God for the gift of salvation through his son, Jesus.

EPILOGUE: POSSIBILITY LIVING STARTS NOW!

Dr. Robert A. Schuller

It has been a privilege to have you as a guest on this journey presented in *Possibility Living*. It is my hope that this experience will be the beginning rather than the end of your adventure with this new paradigm of wholeness. If you choose to continue on this path, you will be faced with many choices. It is my prayer that you make the choices that lead to abundant and prosperous living. It is the narrow road. You will know that you are on the right road when you occasionally find yourself an outcast—the one standing alone away from the crowd, standing for something you know is right. When this happens, don't protest, retreat, or fold. Simply hold your head high and humbly declare the good news of Possibility Living.

It takes maturity, faith, and courage to stand firm for what is right. It is the decision all positive people will need to make. The decision is not one of immediate popularity, but ultimate respect.

IMMEDIATE POPULARITY

Peer pressure is very real and is associated with young people. But the truth is, peer pressure never ends. It is simply disguised better. As we get older, our peers become less defined and more diverse.

Today my peers consist of people in many different realms. I have my fishing buddies, golf associates, people I have met through charity organizations, church members, community acquaintances, and old friends. I find it very interesting to see people in the environment of the church when they are used to seeing me on a boat, on the golf course, or in their store.

If I were interested in immediate popularity, I would change my behavior with each peer group. When I was with my fishing buddies, I would talk and act in a the way they would think "cool." I would become the pleasing chameleon, changing to fit the people I am with. Politicians can be good at this. But the best leaders stand out and get shot at, but never fall over, for they stand on solid rock and are firmly planted. How many times do you have to hit the old oak tree before it falls? The same is true when you choose ultimate respect over immediate popularity.

ULTIMATE RESPECT

I heard this message of "immediate popularity versus ultimate respect" when I was in high school. I went to a mountain retreat and one of our speakers gave us this challenge. I don't know who it was. If I had known I would hold on to those words for the rest of my life, I would have made a note of his name. Words and comments are like that. You never know when the words you say might change a person's life. This works in both a positive and a negative direction.

Rudy Ruddiger, whose college experiences were made into the movie *Rudy*, quit living in the fifth grade, because of the ridicule he received for not being able the memorize the order of the U.S. presidents. He didn't begin to live again until he took hold of his dream, broke out of the steel mill, and moved forward to make it happen. Even though he graduated third from the bottom in his high-school class, he was able to claw his way through the system to the University of Notre Dame.

When he tried out for football he was told, "You are 5 foot nothing, 165 pounds of nothing. We have ninety scholarshiped athletes. Only sixty are allowed to suit for a game. If you expect to put the gold helmet on and run onto the field, you can just put your dreams back in your bag and march out of here." He grunted through several seasons, without any hope of ever being anything more that a moving punching bag for the "real" players. But, he persevered. At the last game of his last year, not only did he run onto the field with his gold helmet, he also played the last 30 seconds and made two tackles. He became the second player in Notre Dame history to be carried off the field. If his classmates and teacher had taught him how to learn instead of putting him down, he would have avoided years of pain. Yet God in his sovereignty knew that without those years of pain, the man of steel, Rudy, would not be who he is today.

Words carve self-images and create beliefs that forge our futures. We have given you words that I believe have the power to change your life and give you the power to succeed in living. Now the choice is yours. Ultimate respect is something that is earned only with time and commitment. This book has the power to help you so that you can make a difference. Keep this book to refresh you. Recommend it to your friends and family. Give copies to those you care about and help me get the message of Possibility Living to those who need it the most. *Anyone can count the seeds in an apple, but only God can count the apples in a seed.*

NOTES

CHAPTER 2

1. Aldrich, Robert A., M.D., as quoted in Fred Barge, D.C., *One Cause, One Cure: The Health and Life Philosophy of Chiropractic*, vol. 6 (La Crosse, WI: Self-published, 1990), p. 81.

2. Eisenberg, D. M., R. C. Kessler, C. Foster, F. E. Norlock, D. R. Calkins, and T. L. Delbanco, "Unconventional Medicine in the U.S.: Prevalence, Costs and Patterns of Use," *New England Journal of Medicine* (1993) 328: 246–52. Eisenberg. D. M., R. B. Davis, S. L. Ettner, S. Appel, S. Wilkey, M. V. Rompay, and R. C. Kessler, "Trends in Alternative Medicine Use in the United States, 1990–1997," *Journal of the American Medical Association* (1998) 280: 1569–75.

3. Tilden, J. H., M.D., as quoted in Fred Barge, D.C., *One Cause, One Cure: The Health and Life Philosophy of Chiropractic*, vol. 6 (La Crosse, WI: Self-published, 1990), p. 15.

4. Mendelsohn, Robert, M.D., *How to Raise a Healthy Child in Spite of Your Doctor* (New York: Ballantine, 1984), p. 77.

5. Weil, Andrew, M.D., *Health and Healing* (Boston: Houghton Mifflin, 1983), p. 76.

6. Palmer, B. J., D.C., Ph.C., *Giant vs. Pigmy* (Davenport, IA: Palmer School of Chiropractic, 1959), p. 24.

7. *Dorland's Medical Dictionary*, 25th ed. (Philadelphia: Saunders, 1974), p. 68.

8. Schweitzer, Albert, M.D., "The Mysterious Placebo: How Mind Helps Medicine Work," Norman Cousins, *Saturday Review*, Oct. 1, 1977, p. 16.

CHAPTER 4

1. Adapted from Palmer, B. J., D.C., Ph.C., *Giant vs. Pygmy* and *The Bigness of the Fellow Within*, vol. 22 (Davenport, IA: Palmer School of Chiropractic, 1959, 1949). The A.D.I.O. principle is extensively discussed throughout these books.

2. Fisher, Barbara Loe, "Shots in the Dark: Attempts at Eradicating Infectious Diseases Are Putting Our Children at Risk." *Epidemiology*, http://www.909shot.com/shotsin.htm.

3. Pert, Candace B., Ph.D., *The Molecules of Emotion* (New York: Touchstone, 1997).

4. Palmer, B. J., D.C., Ph.C., *The Bigness of the Fellow Within*, vol. 22 (Davenport, IA: Palmer School of Chiropractic, 1949), pp. 146–49.

CHAPTER 5

1. Krieger, Dolores, *The Therapeutic Touch: How to Use Your Hands to Help or to Heal* (Englewood Cliffs, NJ: Prentice-Hall, 1979) and Quinn, Janet, "Therapeutic Touch: The Empowerment of Love," *New Realities* (1987): 21–26, as quoted in Institute of Noetic Sciences with William Polle, *The Heart of Healing* (Atlanta: Turner Publishing, 1993), pp. 126–27, 182.

2. Berden, M., I. Jerman, and M. Skarja, "A Possible Physical Basis for the Healing Touch (Biotherapy) Evaluated by High Voltage Electrophotography," *Acupuncture Electrother Res.* 22, no. 2 (1997):127–46.

3. Schanberg, S. M., and T. M. Field, "Sensory Deprivation Stress and Supplemental Stimulation in the Rat Pup and Preterm Human Neonate," *Child*

Development 58, 1431–47, as quoted in Institute of Noetic Sciences with William Polle, *The Heart of Healing* (Atlanta: Turner Publishing, 1993), pp. 143, 186.

4. Aitken, M. J., D. H., C. van Berkel, et al., "Effect of Neonatal Handling on Age-related Impairments Associated with the Hippocampus," *Science* 239 (February 12, 1988): 766–68, as quoted in Institute of Noetic Sciences with William Polle, *The Heart of Healing* (Atlanta: Turner Publishing, 1993), pp. 145, 186.

5. Daniel P. Wirth, "The Effect of Non-Contact Therapeutic Touch on Healing Rate of Full-Thickness Dermal Wounds," *Subtle Energies* 1, no. 1 (Winter 1990).

6. *Nelson's Illustrated Bible Dictionary* (Nelson, 1986).

CHAPTER 6

1. Percival, Mark, *Clinical Nutritional Insights: How Plants Promote Health*, rev. ed. (Advancement of Nutritional Education, 1997).

2. Percival, *Clinical Nutritional Insights*, quoting from Milner, J. A., "Reducing the Risk of Cancer," in Goldberg, ed., *Natural Antioxidants in Human Health and Disease* (New York: Academic Press, 1994), pp. 25–62.

3. Percival, *Clinical Nutritional Insights*, pp. 25–62.

4. Percival, *Clinical Nutritional Insights*, quoting from Biok, J., *Cancer and Natural Medicine: A Textbook of Basic Science and Clinical Research* (Princeton, MN: Oregon Medical Press, 1995); I-San Lin, R., "Photochemicals and Antioxidants," in Goldberg, I., ed. *Functional Foods, Pharmafoods, Nutraceuticals* (New York: Chapman & Hall, 1994), pp. 435–49.

5. Percival, *Clinical Nutritional Insights*, quoting from DiMascio, P., et al., "Lycopene as the Most Efficient Biological Carotinoid Singlet-Oxygen Quencher," *Archives of Biochemistry and Biophysics* 272 (1989): 532–38.

6. Percival, *Clinical Nutritional Insights*, quoting from Franceschi, S., et al., "Tomatoes and the Risk of Digestive-Tract Cancers," *Inter j cancer* 59 (1994):181–84; Giovanucchi, E., et al., "Intake of Carotenoids and Retinal in Relation to Prostate Cancer," *Journal of the National Cancer Institute* 87 (1995): 1767–76.

7. Percival, *Clinical Nutritional Insights*, quoting from Seddon, J. M., et al., "Dietary Carotenoids, Vitamins A, C, and E and Advanced Age-Related Macular Degeneration," *Journal of the American Medical Association* 272 (1994): 1413–20.

8. Clark, Dr. Hulda Regehr, Ph.D, N.D., *The Cure for All Diseases* (Chula Vista, CA: Newdentary Press, 1995), p. 382.

9. Archer, Victor E., M.D., as quoted in Garrison, Robert, Jr., R.Ph., and Elizabeth Somer, M.A., R.D., *Nutritional Desk Reference* (New Canaan, CT: Keats Publishing, 1977), p. 285.

10. *American Journal of Clinical Nutrition* 1999: 69:373–80.

11. Sutton, Brian, D.C., "D.C. online" www.chiroweb.com, 1997.

12. United Press, March 24, 1997. The findings were reported at a press briefing by the American Cancer Society on March 8.

13. Moore, Kathleen, in a presentation to the annual meeting of the Society of Behavioral Medicine in San Francisco, April 18, 1997.

14 and 15. Percival, Mark, *Clinical Nutritional Insights*, vol. 5, no. 4, *Bone Health and Osteoporosis*, rev. ed. (Advanced Nutrition Publications, 1998), quoting from Reid, I. R., et al., "Effect of Calcium Supplementation on Bone Loss in Postmenopausal Women," *New England Journal of Medicine* 323 (1990): 878–83; Adriam, S., et al., "Ipriflavone Prevents Radial Bone Loss in Postmenopausal Women

with Low Bone Mass Over Two Years," *Osteoporosis Int.* 7 (1997):11925; Valente, M., et al., "Effects of 1-Year Treatment with Ipriflavone on Bone in Postmenopausal Women with Low Bone Loss," *Calif. Tissue Int.* 54 (1994): 377–80; Ushiroyama, T., et al., "Efficacy of Ipriflavone and Vitamin D Therapy for the Cessation of Vertebral Bone Loss," *Int. J. Gynecol Obstet* 48 (1995): 283–88.

CHAPTER 7
1. Lenski, C. H., Matthew: *The Commentaries of C.H. Lenski* (Columbus, Ohio, Lutheran Book Concern, 1934), p. 227.

CHAPTER 8
1. As quoted in Shelton, Herbert M., *Fasting Can Save Your Life* (Tampa, FL: American Natural Hygiene Society, P.O. Box 30630; 1996), p. 37.

2. Shelton, *Fasting Can Save Your Life*; Swope, Mary Ruth, *The Roots and Fruits of Fasting* (Lone Star, TX: Swope Enterprises, P.O. Box 1290; 1988).

CHAPTER 10
1. Selye, Hans, "The General Adaptation Syndrome and the Diseases of Adaptation," *Journal of Clinical Endocrinology* 6 (1946): 117–230. See also Locke and Colligan, *The Healer Within,* 62–63.

2. Holmes-Rahe Test.

3. Saudia, T. L., M. R. Kinney, K. C. Brown, L. Young-Ward, "Health Locus of Control and Helpfulness of Prayer," *Heart Lung* (January 20, 1991): 60–65.

4. Smyth, J., A. Stone, A. Hurewitz, and A. Kael, "Effects of Writing About Stressful Experiences on Symptom Reduction in Patients with Asthma or Rheumatoid Arthritis," *Journal of the American Medical Association* 281 (1999):1304–9.

5. Swartz, Gary.

CHAPTER 11
1. McQuay, David, *Orange County Register*.

CHAPTER 12
1. Siegel, Bernie, M.D., *Love, Medicine, and Miracles* (New York: Harper & Row, 1986).

2. Palmer, D.D., *The Science, Art and Philosophy of Chiropractic, The Chiropractor's Adjuster* (Davenport, IO: Portland Printing House), as quoted in Fred Barge, D.C., *One Cause, One Cure: The Health and Life Philosophy of Chiropractic*, vol. 6 (La Crosse, WI: Self-published, 1990), p. 4.

3. Jaffe, Dennis.

4. Ader, Robert.

5. Chung Ha Suh.

6. There are many studies on birth trauma and subluxation. One landmark study is called "Blocked Atlanto Nerve Syndrome," by Dr. G. Gutmann (Manuelle Medicine 25 [1987]: 5–10). Dr. Gutmann, a well-respected researcher who concentrates his efforts on physical medicine, did a study involving 1,000 infants and children with ear infections. His study revealed what he called "blocked atlanto nerve syndrome." The blocked nerves were a result of mechanical misalignment (chiropractors call this condition subluxation) in the upper cervical region. These blocked nerves, he concluded,

contributed to clinical conditions ranging from central motor impairment, lower resistant to infection, and also to increased susceptibility to ear, nose, and throat ailments, which he believes is one of the most common consequences of these upper cervical misalignments. Dr. Gutmann recommends that an examination of the cervical spine should follow every difficult birth, followed by manipulation (adjustment) if necessary. He goes on to say that "the success of adjustments overshadows every other type of treatment, especially the pharmaceutical approach."

Along those same lines, Dr. Gutmann has concluded from his research that up to 80 percent of children are not in autonomic balance; this means that most children's autonomic nervous systems are not optimally functioning. It is important to understand that the main function of the autonomic nervous system is repair, healing, and regulation for the harmonious and synergistic function of all our bodily parts. When this state is achieved, we call it health. He goes on to conclude that this nerve interference is caused by a vertebral subluxation of the upper cervical spine. Another study involving 316 infants suffering from infantile colic found primary upper cervical chiropractic care resulted in satisfactory results in 94 percent of the cases. (Klougart N., N. Nilsson, and J. Jacobsen, Infantile colic treated by Chiropractors: a prospective study of 316 cases. JMPT (August 1989): vol. 12:4.

Life Chiropractic University did a study demonstrating the effectiveness of an adjustment of the upper cervical spine. The study, by Drs. Selano, D.C., Hightower, D.C., Pfleger, Ph.D, Feeley Collins, D.C., and Grostic, D.C., was called "Specific Upper Cervical Adjustments on the CD4 Counts of HIV Positive Patients" (you can find this at the school's Web site). CD4 cell counts of HIV positive individuals were measured by CD4/mm3 in the blood. These tests were performed by the patients' independent medical center, where they were under medical supervision for the condition. The measured CD4 counts in the regular group were dramatically increased over the counts of the control group. A 48 percent increase in CD4 cells was demonstrated over the six-month duration of the study for the adjusted group.

7. Sharp, Virginia A., Alan I. Faden, *Medical harm; historical, conceptual, and ethical dimension of iatrogenic illness*, (Cambridge: Cambridge University Press, 1968) p. 39.